Tracing the Desire Line

A Memoir in Essays

Tracing the Desire Line

A Memoir in Essays

Melissa Matthewson

Split Lip Press

Published by Split Lip Press
333 Sinkler Road
Wyncote, PA 19095
www.splitlippress.com

ISBN: 9781076136138

Cover Art by Jayme Cawthern

Table of Contents

Begin, As Preface   3

Part One: Home   7

Part Two: Break   115

Part Three: Return   183

Appendix: Of Farm Ecology   220

Acknowledgements   223

"When two people are under the influence of the most violent, most insane, most delusive, and most transient of passions, they are required to swear that they will remain in that excited, abnormal, and exhausting condition continuously until death do them part."

—George Bernard Shaw

" That ain't me, that ain't my face. It wasn't even me when I was trying to be that face. I wasn't even really me them; I was just being the way I looked, the way people wanted."

—Ken Kesey, from *One Flew Over the Cuckoo's Nest*

Begin, as Preface

"In memory everything seems to happen to music."

—Tennessee Williams

When I turned 37, I went to the tattoo shop to mark my body—on the right arm where the tender skin below the elbow becomes exposed when the palm faces the sky—a West African symbol that represents the divinity of the earth, or Asase Ye Duru: *the earth has weight.* I wanted an indicator of change, this impulse to commemorate emanating from my own deep instinct to express sentiment as an external embodiment of transformation. The tattoo appears as two brown upside-down hearts resting together—a representation of my identity, my imagination, saying "Here I am," as a badge of desire, an image of dualism too: at the time, I was torn between competing desires: freedom and refuge tugging at each other in the vessel of marriage. I was 37 and living in a mobile home on the side of the highway, away from my children, my farm, my husband, inhabiting the skin of another.

*

Some scholars and activists argue that radio airwaves are a public common and as such, illegal broadcasts should have equal access to listeners as those that have been guaranteed transmission and legal permits. In radio, pirate radio has been a method of empowerment, for democracy and voice. For those who have been disconnected or disenfranchised, pirate radio becomes a mode of expression which represents freedom. As well, in farming, it is often cited that access to land provides a farmer with relative freedom or control of destiny: by working the land with your own hands, you can influence the outcome of your future. Alternatively, in a traditional marriage between a man and a woman, the woman has historically held less dictate over her own destiny; a marriage has been a means for property keeping, or trade of goods, or convenience, with autonomy and agency less a concern for the woman. To say this has changed in the 21st century would be to diminish the fact that women still struggle for identity within the traditional marriage model. For instance, in 1910, anarchist Voltairine de Cleyre remarked that marriage impeded individual freedom for women. Her proclamation resonates, ricochets through eras like soundwaves.

*

I hear in a song "the winter's hiding our desire line," and this short melody, not but two minutes long, weeps broken hearts, builds a refrain through lies, theft, and a fictional woman fucking up over a love affair. I discover then that a desire line represents a path frequently traveled by animal or human, created over time through erosion and repeated use, a system of designing a course from origin to a desired destination. Off the beaten path, so to say. These are the animal paths we want to follow in the forest. The shortcuts in meadows. The quickest way up the mountain. New gaps in places that forgo circuitous journeys. How had I been following my own desire line? Was it possible to design a marriage to foster a self, to explore desire, to be free as an individual woman? Can empowerment be found in both radio *and* sex *and* marriage? What follows then: a story of self, of marriage, of place and how those interact or rub against each other. This is a story of brokenness and return: it follows a line of edges. The story breaks apart—it pauses and punctuates and considers memories, all of them overlapping to create both ruptures and completions.

Part One: Home

1

Fall, or Falling

—Garlic, *Allium sativum*

Gardener's Notes: Manita loam, Class Two; Ruch gravelly silt loam, Class Three; Thompson Creek, Oregon, dry in summer. Josh 37. Melissa 35. Everett 5. Ava 2.

History: Before me, before my son and daughter, roads broke off and ended on fifty acres of grass and weeds, a stopping place for mountain travelers, drifters, pioneers. Before that, the Latgawa and Takelma tribes. I purchased a ten-acre section of this land with my husband, Josh, in 2006. Perhaps we were unhinged hopefuls at the time, optimists, or just young: buying a farm with a house plunging down the hill, bats and snakes living between the walls, the chimney broken, the insulation exposed, the rooms dark and cold. The work, it seemed, was impossible, but what you'll do for ambition. Our neighbor tells us of the settlers who took rest here before pushing over the Siskiyous to California, no small endeavor in wagons and horses. The terrain sharpened into pines, the ride bumpy, I imagine, each man and woman rougher than the one before. Here, horses grazed, licking up cold water to mellow in the shade. Back then, the tenant farmers cut wood and sold it to merchants who hauled it away for dance halls, barns, cabins. All of this I hear from the old man— stripped to the waist, the wear of age striking in the sag of skin bunched around his middle—as he laughs to me in a way that isn't really funny. Only true and frayed. I find evidence too, in the field when I dig, so I hang the relics on our fence as a story—rusty brackets, blades, locks, horseshoe. Josh and I chose this place to name our life, a dream we'd kept in front of us for many years: buy a farm, raise children, work hard, reside. This farm, we said, we'd mold it with our shovels and plow, take the history and create something modern, or maybe, recollect the past, become like the old man next door with the lazy leg and broad smile, all of us on our way to do something important that others might remember.

Culture: Now, at the close of October, Josh rejoices for the dormant world, for the trembling, for the snow. As a farmer, autumn brings a rush of joy, the hope of winter a consolation; he's made it through the heave and draw of relentless work—the tractor turns quiet, the hum of summer finishes. He pulls on heavy boots and drives his truck slower with less push, less fill. Or more, he sits in the driver's seat with engine idling, warming his hands, hesitating in the seconds before he climbs out and runs the crusted grass where there is a layer of ice, a shut gate, and no more light for the day. He drinks two mugs of coffee instead of one, lingering next to the wood stove, scratching his dark beard, considering the year and all that has occurred. He hopes his endeavors have been for something, anything at all. With this comfort of change, then too his heart sinks low into questions as he counts the dollars in his mind and peers at his children in play on the floor. He worries what winter has in store. He senses the cold before it arrives, his awareness grown from the earth itself, though he knows relief in the kill of his fields and the freezing ground. With this transformation, he is closer to me, a companion to hold back the isolation in the darkest days of the year. Or so I hope. Or so I want.

Day Length: This stretch of season progresses in decay. The night settles the day sooner and with stars. All of our work slows. The scent of pine and water infuses the air we breathe. It feels like a tonic, so we take time to walk the farm. Everything is seed heavy—every plant and crop laden with tiny scions of a whole new world, wrapped and hidden in hull and carapace. The fields die back with rot. The bees go. So do the flies. The cold draws out the animals, if only for a moment, temporary, in anticipation of retreat and the blanket of still land. The blue herons appear, harbingers of the coming change, swooping to take their place among the sweep. There are these things too—the fox on the road with a silver-blue coat, thin and hungry. Skunk on the pavement. Bear in the pasture. Geese in triangles over the farm. The salmon in spawn. The deer soon bedding down for gestation. Every animal collects, stores, roams. The hawk cries—enough of this heat, enough of the dry air.

Ripeness: Each day, our farm transforms, the crops in line for storage. We windrow the beans to dry, then shake the plants on tarps, loosening the seeds from their pods, a surprise of rust and maroon swirls on the casing, finished in a luster and shine—the Tiger's Eye. Our son, Everett, picks up the beans, turns them around in his small hands. He asks me, "Aren't they gorgeous?" as he grasps the seed and slips the hardened shell of legume into his pocket. He moves on down the dirt, the sway of his arms like a monkey.

Harvest and Storage: Next to the beans, the flour corn begins to fall sideways, bent over and split in the middle, at the halfway point like a broken and leafy suggestion of surrender. Not total or complete. Like a question mark—as in all that we do on the farm. It is the Painted Mountain kind—multi-hued of burgundy, gold, lavender, rose—the stalks saddled with bran and seed, yellowed leaves. Where I stoop to dig purple potatoes, the birds create a ruckus, take aim at the ears and peck at the seeds, chatter down the corn. It is time to take it home.

Cache: Drying and pungent garlic dangles from old nails in the barn, clusters of twenty pulled from their chancy place in the soil, the dirt caked onto the bulbs, the papery skin flaking off in filmy layers. Soon we will clip the fat cloves from the withering shoot, clean and ruffle the clay, cut for soup, and tuck away for winter. At sunset, my daughter, Ava, and I go to the barn and choose garlic for cooking. I hear the orange tabby mew from another stall. He perches on a tumble of plastic containers, his weight light enough to keep the stack from collapsing. Ava points to the cat, then the garlic, "That, Mommy. That." I reach over my head to pull a bulb from the bundle and put it in her small hands—she takes it to her nose, inhaling, closing her eyes, smiling in that secret way she does. We leave the barn and walk to the house beyond the dying grass with the concrete sky above us. She takes my hand, warm palm and tiny fingers to light my heart. She clutches the garlic in her other hand. The cat follows us, paws padding along the gravelly road behind us. When we arrive at the house, she hands the bulb to her father and smiles up at him. He smiles too and I see the creases of his eyes lift up and wrinkle. He takes the garlic, bends to her proud face and for a moment, rests in that place of love.

Larder: We peel layers of husk from the Tom Thumb's popcorn. My children sort the corn by size, discard the matter into bins and buckets. It all piles up on the stone ground. We settle the grain onto drying racks so the birds will leave it alone. Through the greenhouse doors, wide open to the day, I see the maple down by the creek, far away in its gold light and say, "This isn't so bad, right? Shucking corn together?" A question I hope Josh will answer. He doesn't. His silence measures the depth of his detachment, and I want more. Always more. Everett continues to sort, shows Ava how. He nods to me and smiles. Affirmation, then. The evening comes on. The wind plays out in the shuffling of stock and chaff.

Heritage: I have to remember this is a forgotten tradition—this saving of crops from one season to the next, for the winter ahead. I must remember what we do to preserve. We are like our ancestors in this practice. The Romans built still houses to dry herbs and fruit by fire instead of sun. Cellars and caves stored food as refrigerators do now. Fermentation of barley and fruit made them desirable in their altered state. Nutrition harnessed. Divine supplements of the diet—beer and wine and all. Seed has always been taken in at the end of summer, the corn dried, ground or planted. The beans too. We do less of this preservation now. We sell our corn to neighbors and friends, and that's how we join with our history.

Days to Maturity: At night, the harvest moon rises big and yellow and the fields glow underneath it. I open the window so I can hear the crickets. The night is much too cold for an open window—I leave it open anyway. I want to hear the insects, their sustained rhythm. They are all the night, dominant and about the air. They form a chorus and if I listen long enough and with attention, I hear the harmony of a thousand male octaves, for it is only the boys that sing and rub their wings for the females, for the potential of connection, for attraction— the calling song, the courtship, and then the celebration. It all happens like this outside our windows, good fortune in our witness of such melody. If I could, I'd draw out Josh's voice the same, a proclamation or even a ballad that links us together in his quiet rumination— musings which would draw a picture of these hills, this place, our direction, our own keeping of the day. A song of praise, or at least, conviction.

Wisdom: Instead, together in these days that shorten and nights that become long, under a shimmering moon, we take time to sit with our children as they fall to sleep. The heavy weight of our love fills the room. I feel it as Josh stretches his legs and lays his head in my lap. A spray of cedar and pine hangs from the children's window, tied up in twine with firethorn, a token of our farm's collection of trees and shrubs, something to remind us of the warm season and the world outside our walls. A half put together telescope—a gift from Josh's father—sits on the table while the sky bulging with stars is waiting and the cold moon outside is perched and lingering too, hung in the drifting clouds like the evergreen in the window. I take Josh's hands, feel his strong thumbs, hear the many sounds of our farm home—the clicking of the wood stove as it heats, the yawns and heavy breathing of our children filling the air between me and him, us and them. This is the weight of falling—in love, in farm, in seasons. We must protect and save this substance of surrender, just the same as we fold our farm's goods into bags, boxes, and jars, stored away until we need them again.

Notes and Guarantee: When we go to the neighborhood winery to celebrate the consequence of our year, the vines heave with lush purple grapes. The fruit is ripe, ready for the harvest and crush. The sun glides over the hills as cars move down the road and send dust into the air, covering the ancient and thick grape wood with grit. The ash and pine push up tall into the mountains that fold over the land before us. The peak of hill so far away—I could get there if I had will and time. I could climb it. I know I could. The light turns golden as our children cartwheel over the grass. Blues music pulses into the evening. The sun disappears behind the mountain and we sip the vintage tempranillo, the black grape smooth and fine in our mouths.

We touch the grass with our feet and Josh smiles at me, the sad dark eyes of a man uncertain yet capable of so much. A farmer's eyes, a farmer's glance—look away and hide the years.

Seed Specs: Our narrow valley on Thompson Creek has endured, but barely. The same—our family, the farm, our marriage. All worlds— farmer and wild, woman and man, rancher and cougar—collide with fractured notions and uncommon ground. The salmon used to run up the wide creek, but they don't anymore. The stream dries in summer and everything goes thirsty, even the trees with their deep roots. Our neighbors shoot the cougars when they take the sheep; kill the bears that steal fruit. Some of us hold meetings in stuffy barn rooms to stop the clear-cuts up the road. Some of us fight over water. Some of us still graze our cows in the creek. Some of us—me, my husband—we fumble our way along. We try, on this land, to make it better. At night, when the fires burn in August, the moon comes up orange, its color filtered by the smoke. Everett gasps at the sight, tells me, "The moon looks like Mars! And it has eyes and a mouth too." I see it like he does—ethereal in its altered form. He later takes me down to the lick of creek where he builds a castle of sticks and rocks and leaves. We sit together and listen, the sound of the stream empty now, but soon to be full again at winter's jog.

2

Of

We all want to belong, even if it's a small join, a collective something that we can say yes to—a family, a garage sale, a club like the Girl Scouts where you can ride bikes with bells and twinkle flags, worrying that you aren't going fast enough or that your mother won't see you in all your ponytailed glory as you come pedaling around the corner on a day that is so far away it is hard now to remember. Or how to regard the deep ache of befriending girls who never liked you, the hard suffering of sleepover parties and donut breakfasts. There are people who haven't, who don't, who will never belong—by choice, by sacrifice, or other consequence: a woman up the hill who lives in a salty cabin, alone and tender, opening up once every big moon to show the art she makes, or Valerio Ricetti, who lived in a cave for twenty-two years, carving his own chapel out of rock. Or Noah John Rondeau, who, in the Appalachia mountains, wrote his journals in cipher. Or Despina Achladioti, the Lady of Ro in Greece, living by the water for forty years in a tiny house that must have trembled in ocean storms. How to disregard the longing for human connection? To be wanted? I don't understand this absence, this pushing away of want. To what did they belong: blue water rippling under pinto stars, teepees and wood stacks, pots from sticks, rock gardens and rock walls, tipping trees, hungry birds, scary nights, desire unrequited, and an unbelievable silence settled onto their shoulders, their backs,

maybe their hands?

3

On Coupling

—Black-Tailed Deer, *Odocoileus hemionus*

I never do what I'm supposed to do.

*

For instance, one summer when I was ten, I declared to my mother at
the dinner table, "I'm never getting married." She promptly replied,
"Oh, that's not true. Of course, you'll be married someday." I looked
to the palm trees shivering out back, to my teenage brother sulking
into his plate and argued, "No, I'll never get married." She waved her
hand, brushing aside my disagreement in the way she often did when
she thought I was being silly, childish. At the time, my father didn't
live at home, but in a penthouse apartment near the beach with a lean
woman whose name I can't remember. It's puzzling, maybe illogical,
to think that even then, even in abandonment, my mother would
encourage me to marry.

*

I was a bride for Halloween when I was not yet five. I look at the
picture of myself now with a sort of confused curiosity: I wore a white
train with a crown of fake pink flowers atop my head, a plastic
bouquet in my hands, my small body buried under layers of polyester
with tennis shoes instead of white slippers to match. In the photo, a
parade of costumed children spiral around the neighborhood,

frightened by the vampires and ghosts and tall boys with guns. The sun is as high as it should be at four in the afternoon. I'm not sure why I wanted to be a bride for Halloween. Perhaps because I thought brides were beautiful, elegant, and that's just what I wanted to be when I grew up.

*

Swans mate for years. Sometimes for life. It's an image of true love: swans happily gliding through still water. They stay together through it all—breeding, migration, death.

*

I believed in monogamy for the fourteen years I remained faithful to my husband. I believed because I was in love and thought love would always stay the same, that I'd stay the same. I believed because I wanted to belong. I believed because everyone else did.

*

My parents divorced not long after my dinner table declaration. The day they gave us the news, my brother and I sat on identical couches. A precise light came through the window, into the awkward silence, the blue carpet. I remember wishing to escape, to slip out the door, dip into the pool out back and swim its length in laps, back and forth, back and forth, find a rhythm that might comfort me beneath the palm trees flapping shade, the bougainvillea in bloom, the agapanthus unfolding in bushy purple clumps, their blossoms like open petticoats.

*

After fourteen years, I want to shed the illusion of safety. I want to feel the sensation of new desire, infusing my sexual life with experiment and attention. I don't want to follow the rules of marriage, of monogamy. I didn't have many lovers before Josh. Coming together at a young age, just 20, prevented me from knowing the possibilities of expansive relationships. I didn't understand the limitations of monogamy at 20. I didn't know myself even. A friend, over lunch, flippantly suggests polyamory. I tell Josh. He's not sure what to think. He muses over my idea that maybe we aren't meant for one person, but he doesn't agree. He wants only me. I tell him we could stay married, take lovers, add more depth to our marriage. I say, "Don't you remember the Doug Fir Lounge on our anniversary? The conversation we had in the bar? Who we'd sleep with if we could? Don't you remember the sex afterwards? Remember how you left me panting on the bed?" He says, "I do remember, but I don't care." He looks away, sad, aloof. I'm thinking of the promise of an open marriage. The possibility. Not the risk. He asks me what I'm thinking. I don't reply. He says, "You are so secretive."

*

I create a radio show for a small station tucked into our tumbling range of peaks and hills. I'm one woman playing music in a lonely trailer. One man listens. A man I want. He's another DJ at the station. Others listen too, but it is only him I play for. I think of this as my way to flirt. This man, his eyes reveal a distance I can't seem to reach. His hair is messy, his nature attentive and cautious, slow and subdued.

He'll listen to my voice over the radio from a distance sipping whiskey or beer. I pick music just for him. I don't tell Josh.

*

I wonder about the stories we are told as children. I wonder why no one revealed what marriage would be like: how passion would fade, how domesticity might drown your identity, how money would always be an argument. I remember thinking, *I'll be different than my parents. Love will always go right.*

*

Gibbons exhibit monogamous patterns, though the males tend to wander, fool around, find other females. But despite the drama, most stay, care for their children. The males sing for the females.

*

I want a man to sing to me like the gibbon, a melody unlike any I've heard. Or a man who'll write me letters, tender or violent or both, of longing, of lyric tongue. Something to sway to, to put underneath my pillow and read after dark. I know this: I'm consumed by fantasy, by fairy tales, even though I deny their false truths, their moral messaging.

*

I look to animals for proof that monogamy is an unnatural arrangement. I want their stories to align with mine, to find that they wander and digress so I can say, "See, I'm not wrong! All animals like to screw around." It's difficult to work out this complicated mess of biology, emotion, sexual freedom. There must be some kind of instinctive or innate justification, that what's real and true is our fundamental nature to roam and multi-partner.

*

I'd like to invent a myth of my own, a story of a new woman. She'd be kind and compassionate. She'd live without fear. She'd take walks to the pond and swim with the frogs. Maybe the children would go with her and they'd swim too or watch or laugh while smashing their faces with berries, all of their lips colored in purple juice. This woman, she'd never do anyone wrong, would never have to apologize. She'd wave at the clouds, listen to loud music, make love to a thousand men. She would be a story told around the fire even after her grandchildren were gone.

*

French angelfish are somewhat monogamous in their social structures. It's believed that both members of the couple become jealous when another comes into their territory.

*

I know very little about radio before I begin—I don't know how to work a soundboard, which applications transmit sound through the internet, how to talk like a radio host. What I do know is that music has the potential to communicate over a distance the thing that cannot be said.

*

I read fairy tales to my daughter and I want to change the endings, but Ava already believes in princesses. She imagines her marriage to a future husband, a knight that doesn't exist.

The morning I was to be married, I ate bacon, eggs, toast. I drank too much coffee and worried away the hours alone in my room that I didn't look pretty. I thought maybe Josh would change his mind about me, realize I wasn't all that agreeable. I thought I'd sweat all over the dress my mother had purchased, the cream silk with lace that was too expensive. I thought everyone would notice how the seamstress cut the dress too short, short enough to show my toes. I had never liked my feet and didn't want anyone to see them.

*

I drink bourbon on an eight-degree night and it burns my throat before it warms me, makes me dizzy with desire and love, and I dream about the radio man in my bed at night, imagine what he could do to me while I lay there and let him. It's more than a frozen night. It's a dead night. Everything is dead, the moon barely a glimpse, the ice astral.

*

I met Josh in a beach town in California. I was 19. He had hair of two colors: one side blonde, the other brown. He liked to wear shorts he'd sewn with patches. He was sweet and for a long time we were only friends, though one summer I'd secretly loved him. But he didn't love me then. Many years later, we fell into bed one night after taking lines of cocaine and throwing back beers. We dragged blankets up into the woods to a platform perched in a meadow with trees. The moon was full and he took off my shirt, kissed me tenderly on my chest and shoulders, told me I was beautiful. The sex was awkward, hurried, but there were no expectations. We fell asleep close to dawn, shivering under the down comforter wet with fog, naked and uncertain as to what we'd done, what would now change, how we would be different. I scrambled off the platform when the sun went high, raced to the kitchen for coffee and cigarettes and my best friend who would listen to my doubts.

*

I read novels and essays and poems about women who teemed with desire, who followed their passions. I read everything I can possibly devour: *The Mirror in the Well, a spy in the house of love, Simple Passion, Unmastered.* I want validation from women in literature, like the animals. I want to be allowed to tell lies.

*

Wolves are monogamous, but alpha males have been known to stray.

*

Does nature favor promiscuity? Humans can be socially monogamous, caring for our children, but also searching out other sexual partners. Same with animals: only a small percentage actually remain monogamous, if at all. Maybe they stay together for survival: seahorses stick together when the other has poor swimming skills, but their mating only lasts a season. Or, their brood is so rare they stay together for protection of their young, as in the albatross. John Berger, in his essay "Why Look at Animals?" wrote, "Animals first entered the imagination as messengers and promises." Through animals, we see the passage of our human selves from nature to culture. I wonder if I'm just looking for excuses.

I think about stripping my skin, stepping into someone else. I go alone to a bar to drink margaritas and eat tacos. I don't want to return home. I'm stalling. I know Josh, the loyal and steadfast man, always working, always accommodating, is waiting for me. Salsa music plays on the radio. One server juices limes. The other shuffles food around the cafe, a gorgeous beauty with cropped hair. I greet her, smile shyly. I take off my wedding ring, imagine the bed with her, what it could be like to drink her body.

*

Josh and I make love in the morning with bad breath and warm skin and ice on the window. It happens too fast, but then we want coffee so we leave the bedroom for our cups. I am at my computer on the couch where my fingers are so cold they can barely type the message to someone he doesn't know, someone I don't really know, but who I want to know.

*

One of my father's long-time lovers wore red heels. I noticed the heels at dinner as we twirled spaghetti on our forks. I watched as she crossed her legs underneath the tablecloth, my father's hand moving to her knee while he sipped rosé. I noticed the heels in the car as she climbed out to post an envelope or grab a bottle of vodka from the corner store. I noticed the heels splayed on the floor of the penthouse apartment she shared with my father, the sharp focus of the stilettos waiting for me as I entered from another lonely week at school. A warning. She would slip into them even to go outside to the pool or the garage. Everything about them was full of impulse and inclination, a desire reserved only for my father, for late at night in their bedroom by the beach, along the sea, where they twisted in their sheets. Or maybe I've invented the red stilettos. Maybe they're a way to reduce this woman my father loved to a disgraceful object.

*

I read Rilke's love letters. I wish for my radio man to send me a letter. I want words like Rilke wrote to Lou Andreas-Salomé, a Russian intellectual, in 1897. "I've never seen you without wanting to pray to you. I've never heard you without wanting to place my faith in you. I've never longed for you without wanting to suffer for your sake. I've never desired you without wanting to be able to kneel before you." Do men write like this anymore? Salomé and Rilke blurred the boundaries of love, moving between lover, colleague, protégé, exchanging letters for over twenty-five years, their intimacy changing over time, deepening and widening. I want this to be a model for my affairs: a distant lover in another country who writes me letters I won't share with Josh. I wonder what kinds of intimacy I might cultivate with other men, if it's possible to explore that depth of feeling in any number of relationships.

*

An albatross will cover thousands of miles just to return to the same bird. They even dance for each other.

*

I don't want to be domestic any more. I find this out fourteen years into a relationship, eight years into a marriage. I don't like doing dishes. I'm not interested in how a vacuum works. I had a plan: marry at 28, first baby at 30, second at 34, and now I'm 37 with desires that don't fit the domestic template. Instead, I want to talk late into the night over jars of beer with men whose rules aren't ordinary or conventional, men who are anarchic.

*

Patterns, I tell myself, are for breaking.

*

Andreas-Salomé's lovers included Rilke, Nietzsche, Freud. She wasn't beautiful, but she captivated brilliant men. She rejected Rilke over and over again, but he continued to write to her. I think of what men will do for love. How women make them weak. How was she strong? I can be strong too. I think of Edna St. Vincent Millay, who loved men and women, refused to be compliant in her marriage. Anaïs Nin's affairs defined her identity, her literature, the way she lived. I hope to learn something from these women. I want to know how they lived, if it scared them, if it hurt.

*

After college, Josh and I traveled through Europe. On the coast of Italy, we escaped late at night from hotel rooms to love in bathroom stalls and concrete streets, in between museums and beaches. Maybe it was the air or the Italians, the wine or pot, but we eyed each other over drinks and food and conversation, waiting for the moment we could be alone. This passion exists now only in memory.

*

I stop eating except for nuts, cauliflower, turkey, so the fat drops off me, so I will be able to feel the radio man's hands up the side of my body, over the fleshy but flat skin of my stomach. He's the only thing I can think about. I want him to think about me the way I think about him.

*

When I've angered Josh once again, he stops talking to me, so I shelter in the rural cemetery, sit with Minnie and Richard Cunningham, long buried, their headstones wild with peas. I bring a six-pack of beer, which feels so illicit and extraordinary, and as I drink, I shape out the details of all the angels and stones, thinking how a cemetery doesn't provide any logic to our being in the world, none, but we embrace the place anyway, knowing we'll be in the ground ourselves someday. It comes to me, then, that maybe I'll take multiple lovers as a strategy to avoid death, boredom. I know this doesn't make any sense, but still, I create a map of how I'll quietly upset my domestic life. I check my phone for signs of Josh—a text, an email, a missed call. Nothing. I look around; the stillness of the place unsettles me. No one here but me, the dead, the crickets in the grass, a single bird. I think, *Tonight, this is okay—this discomfort, this avoidance of marital obligation.*

*

Mahimahi mate for life. When one is caught, the other waits for their partner to return.

*

I become convinced I should live as other famous women have lived, that I should construct a marriage in which I can come and go as I like, pursue the interests of many men, maybe women, all the while keeping Josh there to chase off loneliness, insecurity. To maintain a family, but to live independently. I want both: marriage and lovers, freedom and security. I want Josh to say yes to this. Everywhere I go, I wonder about the men I encounter. I judge the nature of married couples, believe they aren't subversive enough, their lives too ordinary. I want to stretch what is acceptable. I circle around the idea that to be a writer, an artist, a real woman, strong and fierce and smart, I must live in a fashion that subverts expectations, that experience can only enhance my life. I don't want to admit this, but this too is a platitude, ordinary in itself.

*

I want to pursue the radio man, but I know this is the most dangerous thing I could ever do.

*

I feel at home in my body now, more comfortable with my sexuality than ever before. I've never thought of myself as a beautiful woman, never took care of myself so men would think so, but here I am, post-pregnancy, post-breastfeeding, intellectual and lean, smart, a woman who men could desire. This truth: new and intoxicating. Men had never wanted me except for Josh, whose love isn't the same as the desire of a stranger.

*

The day we were to be married I thought no one would show up, that we would be standing there just the two of us, no one presiding over the ceremony, no one witnessing. We married each other near the sea, the scent of Monterey pine in the air, the discarded needles cushioning the pathways around the hotel grounds. I walked to the garden after breakfast and saw it dressed in flowers and the warm grass wet with sprinkler mist. Everyone kept asking me if I was ready. I didn't know what to say. I nodded, "Sure, I guess so."

*

I've always wanted to be exceptional, to attract attentions like Edna St. Vincent Millay, who was promiscuous for many years, failing to settle, never wanting to calm into marital life, devoting herself to poetry instead, to experience, to love. She did marry, but to a husband who catered to her dangerous and glamorous life. She was full of posture and strut, utterly beautiful in both physique and language, women and men swooning over her heartbreaks, but ultimately sad. She was desperately dependent on alcohol, and died alone at the base of her stairs with three lines of a poem by her head: "I will control myself, or go inside/I will not flaw perfection with my grief/Handsome, this day: no matter who has died." A lonely and ironic death, her fall from poise and poetry steeped in liters of wine.

*

Prairie voles mate forever, breaking the trend of fickle rodents who prefer promiscuity.

*

It's a temporary tension between freedom and being alone. Caught between two extremes. What's in the middle: buds of a flower, the warp of age in a river tooth, the belly button, a nose, doorways between two walls, Kansas, the hummingbird's beak. The middle is the stronghold, never temporary. It fortifies its sides, keeps them taut, bearing, and complete. But being in the middle is a lonely place. It's a place where the world won't come to your rescue.

*

In Italy, before we were married, we travelled to the five hills of the Liguria region where villages built on rugged terraces of earth perch over the blue sea. These villages are of the sky, afloat and drifting with vineyards and farms on rock, the fruit of tomatoes and grapes drooping over water and boulder. In the village of Riomaggiore, we emptied bottles of thick red wine while sitting on the blue path, the walk of love that led from one village to the next, the road fringed by rue and dusty miller. I embraced my future husband, the sea, the cliffs. We made love, late into the night, under a dark sky mottled with stars and a big round moon, no one but us and our yearning and in the morning our bruises and scraped knees, raw and painful sores on our bodies, the marks of our love, the village ground into us.

*

My father's lover had short hair, thin skin, a smile with no heart. She always called me fat. She rolled her eyes at me. She loved my brother more. He played baseball. Was tall. She whined to my father behind the doors of their bedroom. I would stand outside their room, put my ear to the wood, push my feet against the plush carpet and listen for her complaints. "But you spend all of your time with them," she'd say. "She doesn't like me. She doesn't even talk to me."

*

At night, when the quiet comes and the crickets rub and sail their chitters, Josh and I walk outside to the stars, take out the trash, stand in the road taking in the still and hush of our home. He tells me of his work, how tired he is, how farming ages him, turns him gray. We remember how we built this place, the breaking down, the re-building. He's so kind: before we were married he built a deck for me off the tiny trailer I lived in. He worked all day and when he finished, he carved our initials into the wood. Josh: defined by his work, his devotion. I think of something I read in passing: that searching for another partner when you are married is actually a search for another self. I think of Josh's identity, unwavering in his love, his steady focus on work, on pleasing everyone but himself. I think, *He's selfless. And I'm not.* I look around, to the dying grass, the greenhouses glimmering in the field. We stand there together for a long time. He tells me a funny story of our daughter, the way she dressed herself that morning in mismatched patterns. He's laughing easily. I smile, laugh too. It's easy, this way of being together, but far away, down the road, coming quickly now, I hear the rumble of a truck, and then the headlights—they are flashing through the trees and we move to the side just before it rounds the corner and I tremble as the truck passes me in the night. I'm scared, but I can't see then the way my choices will affect our home, our family. As Josh politely takes my hand, there's no way to know how I'll destroy his heart. Or why that's even necessary.

*

Male mute swans have been known to mess around on the side, even if they do stay to protect the nest.

*

Josh and I fight in a restaurant when I tell him I've written about leaving our marriage, so he leaves me with beet salad and scallops on the way and a half-drunk glass of wine. He sits in the car crying until I ask for a to-go container and grab my teal coat with big pockets, the patrons all looking at me with regret or confusion. Later, after we apologize, he tells me he is overwhelmed by the hurt, but that he can't keep his hands away from my folds.

*

On a friend's porch, someone has left behind a deer skull, beautifully intact, antlers and all, inside a wood crate set up against the wall. I consider the dead skull, the solid antlers, which won't age for ages, which won't die. The hollow sockets where eyes once looked for grass, the empty caves where a nose once bent to dirt. This deer must have lived in the woods behind here, in the fir and madrone, on the hillside taking a bed for its children, laying down in nights cold and rainy like this one. It makes me think about the wild in us all, how it stays tight, how we manage it or don't, how we are animal in our marrow, our depth, our desire for sex as natural as the instinct to build a home, to shelter, to protect.

*

I imagine the radio man's cabin in the rain, laying with him, letting him feel my hips, the light of the blurry day extending its grip on our senses. I want him to tell me his story, while we smell the earth. I want him to know what it means for me to lay there with him.

*

I remember the bar the night before the wedding when the margaritas were too sweet and the DJ called me out as the bride. I remember the day of the wedding hearing people play volleyball outside my window just moments before I was to dress then take photographs and pose. *Oh, isn't she just beautiful? You look lovely.* I remember the woman who did my hair, took the mess of curls and pushed it to the top of my head with too much hairspray. I swore to Josh I wouldn't wear make-up because he loved my face without it, but I did, just a slight gray at the eyelid, a sparkle on the cheek with some gloss to shine the lips.

*

After the children go to bed, we make popcorn we grew ourselves and eat the salty kernels while I drink red wine and stretch my legs onto his lap. We read the first chapter of a novel out loud, my suggestion, the first time we've done something like this. I want to say this moment is significant, but I'm not sure. He looks bored, shortly after I've begun, so I say, "Okay, this description is going on too long." I close the book and go to bed.

*

I speak to him on the phone when I'm away. He says, "The kids miss you." I reply, "I know." And then the distance between us widens.

There isn't much to say. We have fought again on the phone. About the bills. About money. About chores. He misses me so I say, "You'll have to love me fiercer when I return." And he—quiet now on the phone. A sigh. Small and insignificant. He doesn't reply.

*

I want the radio man to grab my hair in the dark and tell me I'm beautiful.

*

When I return home from a trip away, Josh won't touch me. He won't look at me. There is an awkward silence. I tell him, "I'm confined by the construction of marriage." He shakes his head, doesn't understand. I tell him again, "I want experience. I want something different than this farm, this home, these children. I want the world. And that world is other relationships beyond you." He asks, "What's wrong with being married to me?" I say as tenderly as I can, "It isn't you. It's marriage. It's the way it holds me back. I want to feel less guilt in my choices." He's so unhappy. He replies, "But I give you the freedom you desire. What about our vows? Don't those mean anything to you?" I think to myself, *Why hasn't he gone the extra distance for us, for our marriage?* It's been years of negotiations, a constant tug and nag of requests and pleads: less work, more fun, less fighting, more love, less routine, more adventure. I think, *Have I gone the extra distance? What have I done? Am I pulling away because he never gave enough?* I go to him at night because it's what I know. The touch is familiar, the embrace like it has always been, tender when it is, and unfortunate when it's not.

Turtle doves are monogamous. Shakespeare wrote about them like I'm writing this to convince myself that monogamy is something I should believe in. And still, I don't know. Still, I'm riddled with uncertainty. Is this all just a curiosity, a questioning, the way I am in the world: always pushing for something new, some sort of drama to get lost in? It exhausts Josh, this continual upheaval. I want to dismantle all we've created and with urgency. How can I live with this contradiction? Can these desires and needs survive together, coexist?

*

This isn't about love or not love. It's about wanting and desire, to push experience, to know myself through other people, to refashion a new woman, or come back to what I once wanted to be. I believe it's not possible to stay married without this kind of endeavoring.

*

There is one truly sexually monogamous animal: the flatworm, who attaches itself to its partner for life. But this isn't a solution. So I look to the queen honey bee, whose attraction increases with promiscuity, or the dolphin, whose joy in playful sex isn't limited by gender or species, or perhaps the hedge sparrow, whose polyandry defines her sexual life—by courting multiple partners, the bird broadens her range, enabling expansion, expression, possibility.

4

Home

—Wild Forest Apple, *Malus Sylvestris*

The hill that rises behind our home—a lazy slope with broad swaths of headed grass laid thick upon the ground—attracts my son's attention like nothing else on our farm: not the willow branches in their thin stretch to the clouds; not the possibility of an apple from the tree; not even the creek with its frogs and tiny fish. It is the hill that draws his fascination. There on the high ground of our farm, he constructs a fort from a burn pile of discarded wood that was never fully singed. He takes the charred branches and shapes them into a roof, then walks into the shade of our irrigation ditch to collect more sticks. He is proud of his creation. Every day he goes. Every day he wants me there too. "There was a fire here before," I tell him. "When you were just a baby." He looks up from his work, scans the hillside—this pensive boy always thinking, always off somewhere deep in his imaginings—and listens to my story of how the grass burned and the trees came down and the fire jumped over fences, pushing toward the barn. How the day was hot and everything so dry and splintery that the fire swept through the hills swiftly, without choosing what to burn. How I ran out of the house and held him close to me, watching his father aim hoses at the blaze, wondering what would become of us. "I wish I had been older then," he says, then returns to his work, and I see he is thinking about what happens when it all burns.

*

Living near to the ground in this home, I learn how the seasons shape my life, how my land becomes me, but also how I reject it when the demands of the year push my limits and presumptions. When I'm too tired to even sit on the deck and hear the whisper of trees, to hold a book, to play a game. When Josh broods. When the snow caves in a greenhouse. Or a flood carves a new path to the creek. Or the days just don't let go. Despite these harsh lessons, there is much to love. Late spring brings the thread of cottonwood to the air, the tufts of fuzz leaving traces of pollen on my clothes and boots. My hair grows stranded with discarded seed. It is like they become me, or I them, or at least the possibility of a new tree, a restored season perhaps, a remembrance of why we do this at all. The seeds bring with them all that new life, all of which becomes palpable and substantial on my skin, as tangible and real as my daughter's hand or the firm wood of my table. The sky charges with an unlikely illusion of snow, a storm of seed, like stars. Of spring, Aldo Leopold wrote, "One swallow does not make a summer, but one skein of geese, cleaving the murk of a March thaw, is the spring." As the geese make their return to our fields, I walk to the junction of stream and river, where stones spread, gather shore plants—mint, nettle. My dusty farmhouse fills with leaf and stem, the plants twisted and curled on the rafters, twine wrapped around their legs. At spring's end, the salsify seed floats in the air like fluffy umbrellas. They land in my hands and I disperse them too. It's like this: love and not exactly hate, something like doubt.

*

I've searched for home, a place that would require intimacy and a suggestion of knowledge, where I could transcribe experience or at least forge a record of daily life that meant something. To create a foundation of care. I've never wanted to be a nomad, wandering aimlessly into foreign places that challenged my notions of home, though the thrill of wild places beckons me, if even just for the juxtaposition between the need to root versus the seduction of the exotic. Yet, the question nags at me: what does it mean to stay in one place? To ground. To take good care. To give my children this: fixed residence so they will know the willow outside my studio as their shelter for afternoon play, or to locate their bodies in the potato field as base for hide and seek, or to tramp down to the creek for a mid-day bath.

*

In Josh's hands there are seeds, and they tell me stories, bright and old with history. His hands, dark and marked with cuts and veins that pulse under his skin, manifest, making life by his work. They map the places he's been and the tracks of his path, the scrape of fence and the groove of wood. On the underside of his right hand, below each finger, tough and knotty calluses have formed over years of physical effort. He never wears gloves, prefers to feel the sharp pinch of work on his skin, suffering wounds. When he touches me, the farm becomes a part of my body—the twine of peas, the blush of a blossom, the pollen from a tree. His marks become mine. I often mention to him that his hands could break me if he willed them to, though when I say this, his face softens and he mutters, "Never." His right hand grows larger than the left when he clenches them into tight balls, the muscles revealing the frequency with which they pull weeds and cut wood. I like to settle my hands on his, compare the wrinkled soft of mine to the tanned and wide coarseness of his. I love his hands more. They are affectionate, tender, rough, creative. They can build our farm, throw hay and hammer, but too, these hands—responsible, solid, important—they rub our children's backs, stroke tender faces, lift our daughter, cradle the tiniest foot.

*

Everett picks worms from the gravel road during storms, tells me, "Mama, I'm trying to save the worms." He wants them to live. He begs me to watch him save their lives, so precious to him, so dear. I try to do as he asks, but always, the tires of my truck seem to crush their bodies when it's too wet and I can't see the road. It isn't because their lives are insubstantial. It's with the rain the worms come, flushed out from the grass because of puddling, a resultant collection of the thunder clouds. Everett's attention to the worms recalls a memory: I once fashioned a small paper and stick vessel for a neighbor child to float along in an alley puddle. He played for some time, this small boy, moving dirt around the water, the boat perched on the edge of the depression. I remember returning to him throughout the afternoon to watch his progress, to see whether the boat had sailed, sunk or collapsed into damp paper. This was long before I was the mother of a son the same age. The boy took great care with his ship and in his rain gear, talked the day, easing his boat along the water. His mother worried over the fence—the boy was sick, his future uncertain—but he never heeded his mother's calls. It was only the fall of darkness that brought him up from his play and away toward the warmth of hot cocoa and stories. At the time, I wished I could have given him something more, a song or poem to embed the moment in his memory. I wanted to pass on some sort of wisdom he might remember later. I think perhaps he was happy enough with that one simple gift, a homemade toy created in a moment's distraction from a regular day. For him, it was enough. For me, I needed more. But the moment passed.

*

Is a feeling of home the way it becomes familiar in its measurements; say, the sound of cars down by the road, or where resides the finest blackberries? A want for the habitual and customary. For what *feels* right. I want to protect this idea of settlement, and even more so, to give this to my children. Perhaps it's the idea of detachment—of how distance and contemporary life has widened the space of a certain type of understanding, all replaced for diversity of location. Is home knowledge?

*

In summer, the heat anchors itself. This time of year, Everett works his shovel into the dirt. He returns to his fort often, takes shade in the trees where he whistles and whittles and plays the day away. Or he works, side-by-side with his father, pulling up roots and tossing them into boxes for washing. We all do what we can as the temperatures rise, and hope that fire won't burn the hills.

*

I take shelter in the shade of the plum and apple trees, lying against the dry grass, nestling Everett into me to watch the sky move in all directions, but mostly east where the clouds go. Or sometimes the sky shifts into an empty container, and there are only the birds—the warblers, sparrows, blue jays, sometimes chickadee—and I think the world is so big, so huge to hold this much beauty. The impermanence sad, like the way I'll never forget how my boy runs the gravel road in the throes of summer, the world unfolding for him in every direction. The beauty just as temporary as his tiny smile. I want to capture this, somehow push it all into a jar and set it on my windowsill to watch the way light reflects off its ceremony, but the light stretches the day and I cannot stop time or the trace of evening. So I go to the lower field and wash my hand over the fading orchard grass. I look to see that everything is hungry, even the trees wallowing in the heat. We harvest each day and put up all that we cannot eat.

*

As the season shifts, everything becomes active and alert once again. A steady pace of rummaging picks up as the hawks present—their pitched cry echoes outside my windows. They know how everything changes. They are searching just like the rest of us. The skunks come out from their hiding places and hunt for their winter homes. I find them flattened on every road, their odor wrenching my nostrils. I can taste the smell in my mouth. It lodges in my throat, their deaths a reminder that we must watch closely as we move across the land. And then everything quiets itself in preparation for winter, toward sleep and rest as the dark months approach. Everett helps to collect kindling, toss wood in piles, begs to chop with an axe. He's always eager to labor, to help, to be a part of the work of our farm. We make plans for winter together. We build fires in the stove. We collect rose hips for our tea. We do most of this without Josh. And together, we see the world take on a new look—colder, crisp, open. The trees feel it too. The incongruity of the season—the abundant harvest along with the decline—sharpens our senses.

*

Once, a buck wandered into the open gate of our two-acre field. It grazed on grass and discarded field mowings. Our dog took after it, ducking under the narrow hole in the tall fence, running to the field where she chased him, tiring the animal with her resolve to take rack and hoof. The deer vaulted back and forth across the field, frightened, knowing it had been caught. The deer had nowhere to go, though we opened the gates; we tried to release it, to show it the way, but in its panic, the deer collided with the fence, jumped and twisted its neck in the wire, falling with a quick drop of finality. I took Everett to see the deer's body, to teach him about this life and this death. The deer was warm still, its life slowly leaving it, soon to turn cold, its heart released of blood. We could have left it. Something would have come, slowly over days, one animal, then another, until all that remained were bits and pieces of flesh and bone and tufts of fur. Instead, we stripped the deer in the yard, lit a candle for its soul, ate its meat in our stew.

*

Humans have always wandered, searching for the best place to call home. Our curiosity for distance supplants a desire to stay: what's beyond that horizon, or what rough shore may I climb today? Does staying become a provincial decision? Culture adheres negative connotations in choosing to stay—words like parochial, insular, sectarian define the rural homesteaders—but what if we strayed from this definition and instead, designed a pastoral reformation, restoring value in staying home, making ignorance not a result of the choice to remain, but an intelligence unlike any other? And, to that extent, to take apart that which presents as a dichotomy of maps: maps are a guide to the unknown, to be understood in lines drawn and connected. Maps provide us with a mastery of where we are and where we want to go, but what if we changed that map to include the wisdom of home, to draw out the live oak or the canoe asleep in the woods, the landmarks notable to only a few, as in memory maybe? What if the common sense of place was as beloved as experience of cultural and global diversity? Wendell Berry writes that "the world cannot be discovered by a journey of miles, no matter how long, but only by a spiritual journey, a journey of one inch, very arduous and humbling and joyful, by which we arrive at the ground at our own feet, and learn to be at home." And maybe this is what I desire most for my children, and myself, this idea that Berry has suggested—that we learn how to remain among the clutter of contemporary life, that wit and insight grow from a country of years spent in one place.

*

When winter comes, the cold settles in dry and deep. The sun rests low on the horizon bringing the light in slow, warming me just a bit while the day is high. I shift my work and move slower as the cold reaches through the weave of my sweater and covers my arms with a blank chill. The trees sleep, bare and stripped, just their wood is shining and the maze of branches shelters the ground. I crunch leaves and sticks when I walk, find acorns stuck in the mud and gravel. I take Everett with me in the cold. He finds what he can: a rock here, a stick there. Ice crystals form on the snow, pointed and sharp, reaching for the sun that comes so late in rising. Everett bends to touch the ice, collects treasures for his pockets. The ground glitters before us. When the temperature dips below twenty, there are no birds, only the sound of the creek rushing by and our boots smashing ice. The burn pile grows taller with each day and if I wanted to, I could light a match to it, bring another fire to warm us, keep the animals in their hiding places. When the rush of cold air comes down the mountain, the woods become us, our surrounding, and we make of them our winter story.

*

Recently, Everett whispered secrets to me at his bedtime, his little legs and arms tucked under heavy blankets as he floated in the air, his bed hung above the floor, supported by wood, screws, and nothing else. With his eyes closed, he said to me, "Mama? I have something important to tell you. And kinda sad."

"Yes?" I replied.

"I found a dead bird at the barn today."

"Oh."

"Papa and me buried it. I held the shovel."

"That *is* sad. What kind of bird was it?"

"A blue jay."

Quiet.

"I like blue jays," he said.

"Yeah, me too."

I know then, standing in the dark while he rests above me, that I give him the farm in all of its chaotic abundance, luminous in its diversity of plants and animals. I guide him in his growing awareness of the physical world as he adapts and matures his senses over years of experience. I give him a home that will shape his life in wonder, gather fortitude, bring influence and possibility. He is eager for sensation. I want to tell him that we always keep our homes with us, that we carry them along with us wherever we go. I want to tell him that all of the mystery and prayer of each place we live, all of it creates its own heartbreak and calls to mind the things we miss. I want to say all of this as he falls asleep, but I know he is still too young to understand. I do not speak these things so he can discover them.

*

I think this just might be right. All that does not dissipate—the shifting timber, the dark places, our homes, seeds, forts, hands—they carry our stories. The leaves must hold the weight of memories. I know they do. Some memories we let go, others we take in, and cup, nurture. Like how the blue herons come in the fall—they move along the fields graceful and slim like some great beauties resting in the grass. They take stock, composed and placid as glass, while the leaves mix around them, distributing what they will on the wind.

*

Over the season, the blackberry has crawled up and over Everett's fort. The vines create shade, cover the roof and entrance, but also forge an impenetrable layer of thicket that he cannot move past. Frustrated, he abandons it, pursues something more defined, easier to access, and open to the light of day. Closer to home. He is fickle as boys will be. Under the shade of our oak and pine, he says to me, "The world is so beautiful" and he raises his hands in the air as if he is conducting a piece of music, his thin body rocking in his shoes. He hears the music of his small world in a thousand different melodies. From him, I learn how the wood feels under his hands and feet when he climbs—barefoot, proud, and brave. He runs the stroke of his own dreams while the love of the world wraps around him like his blankets, like the snug safety of his home, like the farm and its trees, like his mother's warm body.

"I can still see the trees, Mama, but they are almost gone," he says as we push firewood in a wheelbarrow toward the house, the last light just about to disappear.

"Yes, honey, I see." I listen to him more than I talk. I think this is a wise thing to do.

He looks up at me and says, "Thank you for making the farm, Mama. Papa, too. I really love the farm." He waits for encouragement—he is always searching for the recognition he desires.

I smile and nod.

We walk together past the slanted red barn and its tin roof and the rotting posts that hold it up. Past the wood chips and decaying compost and to the house, which keeps the rest of our family and the things we love—the stand-up piano pushed up against the dining room wall, the books in stacks on the floor, all of them tumbling over each other, the titles fading on the spine, the paper just another manifestation of wood. The hats and sweaters, the canned pickles, the photographs and art framed in black metal and wood, the heavy quilts, the play capes and swords. And there also, down in the basement, tucked into the file cabinet drawer, the deed to our farm with map and survey lines, rights to water, covenants, and use drawn out—the official record that tells us this is our place, our home, our farm that will sketch its hills onto Everett's hands as he grows.

5

Of Family

When my daughter wasn't even a real thing, just a hope, and my son
fit between my arms, the wall outside their bedroom was papered with
sheets of pink and white stripes. Josh and I tore it off, finding
newsprint underneath, and beautiful splintered wood, lengths of pine
nailed together with crooked iron. We left the bits of paper on the
storied wall, the wood too, exposing a window into the past, to what
was gone of this old house and the people who had dreamed here
before us. A laminated map of our bioregion hangs on that wall now,
the terrain all wild and sharp and full of beautiful edges. At night,
when I put my children to sleep, I listen for Ava's breath, Everett's
sighs, the slight air pushed from their throats into the space between
us. Ava curls with her toy animals—a knitted turtle, a plush pig, a
hand-made doll. Everett is buried under blankets high above the
floor. Out their window, I see the stars rushing toward a new morning,
blurry and distant shapes scattered above the rooftop. I wait to hear
for the dreams coming over the children, swallowing them like a
cloud. The wall holds my children safe for now, one of many walls
we've finished that I know cannot contain them forever. Everett says
to me, "I'm going to live with you always."

6

Of Discontent

—Tall Fescue, *Festuca arundinacea*

Live in each season as it passes; breathe the air, drink the drink, taste the fruit, and resign yourself to the influence of the earth.[1]

I'm at the deck with a drink, the day now settling into a comfort of twilight. Soon, a haunting of shadow arrives with an increased murmur of night sound. Five, for me, is an intersection. I sit regularly with its substance of light and not-light. For years, I've always appealed to its value as a time of day. Five o'clock: a glad time for the clutch of birds on the fence. I love the farm at this time of day, more than any other hour. Animals scatter. The coming dark inspires quiet, forces us to quit working. Now, I think of palm trees in my father's yard falling over brick, over planks into the neighbor's court. Also, leaving home in a car by the horse ranch with all the jasmine, creeping fig, primrose. Two bonsai in front. The lawn all square with grass. As long as I can remember, I've roamed with agitation, unease; even now, as I wait for the colors of sky to turn up for one more showing. I'm probably rolling around in the fescue, or at least laying out a few books, pretending to read, highlighting long passages in pink. I've drunk, am

---

[1]   *-in reference to Walden, from Thoreau*

drinking, dinner just a thought, not a plan. I've put on a sweater to warm my arms, the contours of dusk taking over, those neat chatters of a farm or a yard's evening hunt. I visit with myself at nearly every five o'clock. The sky lavender, peach, like I could eat the stream of color over the rise, like it might taste of fruit or herbs. Five belongs to those who might water it with affection, who know that to move at this hour is a thing of opposition. Instead, a stillness is required, unlike the pace of nine, or even ten, or at the cliff of a new day, the other five, the other shadow break.

Things do not change; we change.

At midnight, I'm mostly pining, laying on the bed, covers pulled over me, brooding. Josh has fallen asleep on the couch again, still in his work clothes, hands stained and streaked with dirt. I take a drink of water at the sink, look through the cabinets. At this hour with the deer bedding down and the raccoons making the dog bark, I can't help but think of all my desire bottled up like fizzy water that's going to blow at some point, shoot up over the tops of all these trees. I know at this hour, desire is an impossibility not to be mentioned at the dinner table, or among friends while over wine and cheese and all manner of practicality. Desire is for midnight in the dark. I hear Josh breathing in the other room, his back tired and muscles taut, his dreams becoming lists of tasks and chores.

Only that day dawns to which we are awake. There is more day to dawn. The sun is but a morning star.

In the morning, I'm at the deck with birds. The morning is still unheard, not a notion of what could come, but a pouch of possibility, an opportunity, an entrance. Five, for me, a beginning. What will the day hold? What can we achieve in our work? What will I reject once again: farming, parenting, responsibility? I think how hard it is, sometimes, to even move about in the morning, the reserve of energy needed to pursue a new day. Isn't this day just a shadow of the day before? If at this hour anything appears, it is the sounds, adrift, moving. This time is for the birds and collages of interminable progress, a spreading out. I want to create something here at this time of five, a machine of lichen, branch, stone, a small landscape that could churn out new things for children to play with, or something that lists words upon the air like flashes of stories that tell of the good things to come, because there's always that hope.

Morning brings back the heroic ages. There was something cosmical about it; a standing advertisement, till forbidden, of the everlasting vigor and fertility of the world.

A summer storm comes in at nine. A steady rain falls with the blue jay beaking away outside, picking up worms, taking seed. Josh works in the barn. My children are away at school. I won't go out today. I won't work, though the work defines the rhythm of our days. Every day.

Each day. I look at the books on my desk scattered about like leaves or last night's clothes stripped to the floor in a tender moment. We left them there to dirty. I hear the birds talking to each other out the window, the air trembling with some sort of pull or shift. I sense the revision in all things, in the wasted time, in the sharp pang of regret. At nine, in my room, alone, when my fingers work their bone and skin, the purposelessness of some days is persuasive in the way my tired legs drift about the wood floors of this old farmhouse. In this instance, at this nine, the light has come down onto my bookshelf from the window, and my wild mind tips and tilts, considering the heart, the way I'll choose to break my husband's. It is these mornings, I think, the heart could be a raw, dead thing laying in the road waiting to be rescued, or picked about by a bird in all of its fall hunger, waiting now for the cold to come and kill everything around.

I have, as it were, my own sun and moon and stars, and a little world all to myself.

It's mid-day and I'm in the yard with the grass, matted where the dog has been resting. Smoke has blown in over the mountains from California. Nothing really moves at this hour. We're all subdued, the animals included. It's time to tidy the yard or take a nap like the birds who are also nesting. Today, I let myself go—I don't want to come together. I don't want to meet any expectations. I watch the dog excavate and harrow, intent for a gopher, or some other varmint. A plane cruises above. It disturbs the noon subdue. I think of Josh miles away at the market, selling vegetables, making money for our family. I doze a bit waiting for the sound of a dead gopher struggling in the clutch of my dog's jaw on its way to death. When I open my eyes, the dog is deep into the ground. He won't budge until the animal draws out and he can rip it to shreds, paw at it. The apples are almost ready. I see them beginning to detach from the branch, the fruit rounded in crimson and perfectly ripe for the first bite.

In any weather, at any hour of the day or night, I have been anxious to improve the nick of time, and notch it on my stick too; to stand on the meeting of two eternities, the past and future, which is precisely the present moment; to toe that line.

It's midnight again and I'm wondering about a man. I haunt my house like a ghost looking in on the children while they sleep, sad always when I see them—I don't know the pain that waits for them. Thunder at this time of night comes down over the house like a charge, like a bull, like something about to take my house away, maybe blow it to the top of the mountain, landing where I climbed the peak not too long ago with another man, the man who thinks I'm beautiful and interesting. We rested there on that mountain to stack rocks, eat cheese, grapes, cucumbers, talk ruination, philosophy. I open the window to witness such rage. I open the window to hear the thrust of the world and its sorrows. I look for a blaze, the dry hills blistered with bushes too dry to mow, dry enough to spread fire like a blanket of crimson wings, but I can't see in the dark.

7

The Shank

　　　　　　　—Pacific Treefrog, *Pseudacris regilla*

We left dinner cold on our plates to meet the shank of day. As we climbed the hill—my children and I—we stopped near the pond, just on that edge between slope and perch, the willow branches all fiery and orange and long for the day, and I wanted them to put their ears to the ground, to hear the earth swallow, to listen to the night and the hum of a million tiny organisms working to grow the trees, but instead, in the twilight of a March day, we listened to the frogs. A hundred or more groans and belches and tones. We listened because we couldn't listen to anything else, the frogs having interrupted our original occasion for setting out. We listened because I wanted my children to hear the row of a day's end, of nightfall, of what makes our place sound out and brush the sky with song. Everett swung a branch against the dry grass, which now, under a prolonged length of day pushed up new green. Ava shushed him, as I did too, and put her head to my shoulder and smiled at the ensemble. "Do you hear," I said to her. "Do you hear," as if she could not, as if her experience would be different, both of us so fully aware of the cacophony of voices around us, the oasis of octaves—alert, alive, and rupturing the air.

My father always said the shanks of day were best—that time just before dark when the horizon softens into a tinge of color, when the day unwinds and work has been left behind, when a drink could be poured and sipped with polite conversation. Funny to think a shank is like a shaft or stem of nail, spoon, key, anchor, fishing hook even, or the port-braised shank of a lamb. But I think the longer stretch of shadows is a better fit—the remainder, the last of something, what is almost gone, the lingering light, the gap between what was and what will be.

It isn't the only time I have celebrated the dusk. Years ago, pulling on smoke while playing songs on a dark porch, the fried odor of souvlaki simmering in from the Greek restaurant next door and the rattling hum of the bouzouki haranguing through the open windows, I watched the day go. I could hear the cafe's owner, Vasili, dancing on the wood tables and a chant of "Opa!" as wine glasses clanked from table-to-table, retsina spilling across the plastic floor. This happened at least once before nine, before close, before the tired cooks and servers turned off stoves and untied aprons. I continued to strum my old guitar until my Moroccan neighbor pulled into the driveway next door, his four children descending on him as he climbed from his silver Cadillac, arms loaded with bags of groceries, soda and candy, a mix of chaotic voices jumbling under the new stars, even his dog and cat appearing from the yard. Within minutes, I'd hear the drumming commence, the beating of one man's hands, the rhythm of the coming night.

And then, from the smoky blur of the now gone day, I made out the wings of a pigeon picking bits of sloppy discarded meat on the concrete across the way, the glow of the McDonald's fluorescents illuminating the bird, the grunge, the trash cans, and the passing cars making their way where—to the shore, to the roar of the ocean nearby, over that way, by the stony cliffs of a college town doomed to someday fall into the sea.

Yes, everything is so active toward the shank—a true buzzing of enterprise and experience. The day disappears into shadows like little cloaks sheltering the suggestion of night. And at the rise of morning, I wait for it. The shank pulls me to it, beckons me to go outside, to engage with the hems and bulk of my home, to listen and to know, and more, to explore its vague boundaries with care and curiosity. I know this: porches were created for the shank. Van Morrison too. His music sings the half-light and so this: there isn't anything I know better than the dusk, a drink, a porch, a swath of trees, the man I love, and Van Morrison smoothing out the rough edges of night that always arrives, reliable and sure in its congregation.

And Dad, how he delighted in the last of afternoon, that place in time when the bottle came uncorked, the dry fruity smell of wine released into the kitchen as he poured my mother a glass. The ending day drew him into a quiet peace where he studied my face, his daughter, the mystery of his own brood. What did he make of this girl with her broken heart and sulking tongue? Of this girl with spirit and fire that rose straight up from the ground through her toes and thighs to the very top of her head? As he sipped his wine and puffed his smoke, the day ended, the yard of birds quieted and the crickets huddled in the patch of grass next to where we sat, and he must have thought, this youth, this gap of age stretched out between us is nothing really, nothing but a great silence and a vast field of desire never fully realized, and all that was left was the shivering palm trees at our backs, their shanks crossed fiber—joined, thick braids—trees that would extend their trunks slowly, until something or someone would strip their skin, like stranded filaments of palm and shank, scattered shreds at the last of day.

8

Of Bar, Desire

I'm not from here, but you know that. This is just a bar on the water, a glass of grappa and warm olives on the table in front of us. I can't make out the sharp cut of your jaw in the low light. I can't see it like I can when the afternoon shows it to me. It's just that we've been talking, but I do most of it while your eyes follow my lips then look away to the bar, a beautiful platform for our hands, our drinks. It must be that you're shy. I'm trying to work that out while we talk. We don't know each other well and I'm nervous because you're beautiful and smart, so I'm talking quickly while you shake your head in agreement I suppose. It's only later I hear about your broken heart. There are dead animals on the wall too—a skunk, an ox, many deer—and the music isn't good and too loud and the popcorn has rosemary, smoked salt, and ground porcini mushrooms sprinkled on it. It could have been easy to plant a kiss on your lips, but then my breath might be porcini and salt with a relish of red wine, and that'd be just the thing to remind you how much you miss her. What she tasted like in your mouth. I want to tell you about my desire. I want you to tell me I am beautiful in the bar light. But the city, I see it's lonely, just like you, just like me: the abandoned nest I found in the empty branches of a tree; clouds gathering over my head; empty sidewalks except the man smoking a cigarette under the awning; a sign that says Lenora, the middle name of my daughter, or close enough to Lenore to make me think of her; the woman throwing up under the stars; the giggling drunk in the bakery; the empty whiskey glasses; the feigned gestures of women in high heels. I tell you all this, and also, that I didn't even go to the Ferris wheel or to the water or shop for apples at the market. I did, however, walk with you against a mean wind and up the stone sidewalks that seemed like they could go on forever, the rain holding off for just a few more minutes until we landed safely inside the bar with the loud music, the popcorn, the drinks and our knees nearly touching.

9

Notes from the Underground, or the Narrator as Rebel

Start with the word catholic and an image surfaces—what first? Brother Aquinas adorned in black robes, his large gold cross (or was it silver) swinging from hip-to-hip, his cloaked arms holding the Bible tight to his chest, in reach of his heart. Never a novel, as in *A Portrait of the Artist as a Young Man,* which we read together in those subdued periods after lunch: *I shall express myself as I am. I will not serve that in which I no longer believe.* He assumed a wry smile, knowing something I did not, nodding to me gently as he passed the school's lawned grotto with Mother Mary balanced on the brick stones, the stations of the cross headlining the campus green. Now, when I run my finger along the thesaurus entry, I cut to the shared synonyms— *catholic, see also: tolerant, cosmic, liberal, broad.* Latitude even. Is that not freedom?

Start with the word speech, of utterances, of expression. As in this story: it's 1990 and I'm thirteen, awkward and fiercely devoted to both Walt Whitman and Kirk Cameron. Pop culture and poetry, side-by-side. It's 1990 and I'm waiting for something to happen, anything, reading the news: Nelson Mandela walks free, touching his prisoned feet to the brown earth, in exaltation, in grief; in England, Manchester inmates riot, closed up and bolted into the prison chapel, spreading out to the pews, the contrast of their orange garments sharp against fine wood, for what: freedom. *I will try to express myself in some mode of life or art as freely as I can and as wholly as I can.* In this, I begin to write short essays on private school, plaid uniforms, adolescent rage, compile them into an illegal newspaper distributed at lunchtime on the quiet lawn, the noon light stripping the trees into corrugated shadows, all that stunning bougainvillea and ceanothus murmuring with spring. I type out the words with my friend K in her dark bedroom, the suburbs quietly massacring the orange groves out the window, this friend K who introduced me to Virginia Woolf and revolution, whose Vietnamese grandmother was so beautiful, so small, cooking stews all afternoon and drinking foreign teas from tiny saucers, the rose garden out back alive with thorns and bees and any number of wild shrub or insect. We call it the *Underground Pravda,* so named after a Soviet paper. My father copies the tabloid on Sunday at his EF Hutton office, the desks empty of brokers and agents for now, the still air of the economy on the precipice of waking up to a new stock day. Read: *Congress shall make no law abridging the freedom of speech.*

Start with the word private, then add school, then the Sisters of the Company of Mary, Our Lady, an order whose mission unfolds its history like a straight bar from the slopes of Bordeaux, all the spokes of their vocation pointed toward the individuation of a girl. And that's a fact until you add the thinking mind and all its impulse and intellect. *I am not afraid to make a mistake, even a great mistake.* Add to the curriculum my English teacher, Mr. Rewald, who said the word dissent, who storied the afternoon with nature versus nurture and the wild call of wolves and bad men who beat their animals into submission, who reminded me that those trees out there are fierce with the possibility of beauty, who said power in art, who said write a line that lessens the distance between us, filling the lonely gaps with stories too many to count.

Start with expel and continue with tyranny by the school government and the disapproval of the rector, whose fame was but a Hollywood actress for a niece and a stance, tall and mean. Start with severity, of a rule system not devised for fracturing by the design of two young girls who only set out to create something unique and individual. Who only wanted to write: remake the ordinary of daily life into something beautiful, structure their imaginations, maybe grow them, just a bit different from the other students. No, rules are rules, contrived not to be broken. *In the wide land under a tender lucid evening sky, a cloud drifting westward amid a pale green sea of heaven, they stood together, children that had erred.* All this, followed by a final goodbye from the literature teacher, who requested a meeting in the empty classroom, the room now curved into a posture of disappointment, its chairs formed into an open build so that discourse grew from its shape—a blueprint for eye contact and speaking history under rotating fans instead of backs set up for divine rectitude. All this, followed by the hammering of the Constitution by my father, advocating for rights and justice, for freedom, that word so related to—

Catholic.

End with the antonym, of which is narrow. Limited. Insufficient. Still, this doesn't parse out: how to understand a word so separated from its common usage in the context of this story, so paradoxical, so contrary. Instead, shove the word out entirely, or go back to its origin from the Greek, *katholikos*, and say, this is what we desire as universal: a vision of art both progressive and true, of open craft and limitless words, outside of institution, outside of rule.

10

Of Rings

I lost my wedding ring on an early Saturday morning, two years into our marriage. I was walking from the barn to the house, early morning, before dawn, to start up the Ford truck for the farmers' market when I noticed the ring was no longer on my finger. Josh had designed the platinum ring himself with an artist over many months, the gems inset so as not to catch my curly hair. The diamonds originated from his father's family: his great-great-grandfather's tie pin and his great-great-grandmother's wedding ring, the story of the gems significant—his great-great-grandfather escaped the Russian army into Germany then immigrated to Ellis Island; his great-great-grandmother sheltering her wedding ring on the windy streets of Chicago as she settled into her new role as bride. I lost the history and I didn't know how. I looked everywhere, even rented a metal detector, but never found the ring. It's buried now in the gravel of our road, or washed into the sewer. Gone. What are the meanings of these objects of obligation, and to what did it matter that I no longer wore that particular symbol of marriage? Wedding rings are an announcement to the man at the bar looking at you that your commitment to someone else is public, real, meaning he shouldn't talk to you, but says who? The shape of a circle signifies forever. As a gift, perhaps, an exchange of love, mine given to me in a meadow of grass and lupine high above the sea on a December night, the sky scratched with stars.

11

Of Opening

It's likely Josh and I were sharing a cocktail when we decided to open our marriage—tequila, ice, and lime. We'd been together for fourteen years, married for nine. We had a farm, two children, and I thought, instead of cheating, maybe we could explore sex with others if we talked about it openly. If we didn't hide, which is what it seemed to me the majority of couples did. He reluctantly agreed to think on it. I went about sending him articles, buying books, talking to friends. I was determined to convince him this was a good thing to do. I wanted it badly. More than him. One day he returned home from dropping Everett off at school and he smiled, told me, "I know who I want to pursue."

C_ was the 4th grade teacher at Everett's rural charter school—thin, petite, athletic, beautifully innocent face. She attended my gym, and I'd often see her come down the stairs from morning yoga with a look of bright ecstasy. She was farm-girl pretty. She was freshly-showered pretty. I really tried not to hate her. That was the deal Josh and I had made: no jealousy, no hate, all trust, all openness. That word—open. As in exposed, without secrets, without shame. Public.

Josh transformed into a nervous school boy around C_, crumbling into incoherence without poise. I'd never seen him like that. The man I loved and married was confident, critical, determined, a work horse—these characteristics part of my attraction to him. To watch him fall apart over a woman, not me, was unlike anything I'd ever experienced. I felt a mixture of fascination and envy.

He first talked to C_ at the school picnic before the start of the new year. End of August, angry and hot. When we arrived with our children in tow, he turned to me, "There she is." She was dressed as a teacher should be—long skirt and pretty blouse—but I could make out the thin frame of her naked body underneath the billowy shirt. I pictured her vagina under the cotton of her panties. I felt another pang of envy rise up. I pushed it away. I smiled to Josh as I ushered the children to the picnic shelter. "Go talk to her," I encouraged. He looked at me uncertainly. "No way, I can't. What would I say?" he asked.

As families filled the picnic shelter, the potluck line wrapped around the tables. We sat with other parents. My children ran off into the grass and down by the river. Josh watched C_. I turned to him, gave him a plate and fork, and nudged him toward the line. "Go," I said. I watched as he stepped behind her. When she turned to greet him, they began to talk and I could see him awkwardly grab food while trying to maintain eye contact. He smiled a lot. Nodded. He never once looked my way.

She surfs, he told me later in the car, our children asleep in the back seat. I had so many questions. What were the ethics of dating a teacher? Is that acceptable? Will she be open to dating a married man? Can anyone know? What if people see them together? Will he sleep with her? Will she be more beautiful than me? Will he fall in love? He took my hand on the drive home—I was looking out the window, considering the trees, sad, lonely, and he recognized my shift. I tried to push the feelings down—this was my idea in the first place. It's just fantasy and play, I thought. We're just trying something new.

12

Of Paris, A Long Time Ago

It was the Seine after all—birds and pigeons and old stone bridges. At 22, I smoked and sauntered with my pack, the bag riding the top of my hips. It felt good to have that weight pushing down on my bones and skin, moving about my hips such that a man could take notice. I thought about the statues and about nothing at all, really, but that this was Paris. I was young with a pocketful of money, and there was nothing to call up or remember during my walk along the Seine. I was not yet married. I was not yet taking a lover. A tall, black man, full of dreads, approached me. Quelle jolie, he said as I straightened my back, adjusted my shoulders, smiled. Bonjour, I said, watching as the water rolled through the gray stone of the city and then back at him as he curved his head. I marched on to the Musee d'Orsay to look at art I didn't care about, the day having just begun over all the simple things we do to start a day—tea and biscuits and a paper, or a walk through the morning market when the French farmers call to you for their bread, for their vegetables, for their love. I haven't forgotten him, nor the feeling of being lifted up like that, as if I could swim the Seine without opening my eyes, feel the pull of my young muscles in the current, or fly over the brick and parks and old men playing chess on the street, my body fanning out through the clouds, then dropping to the next alley over where a woman embraces a man against the brick wall of a cafe, or butcher shop, or bakery with just the scent of croissant and trash and coffee mingling in the Paris air as they kiss and he touches her hair and I watch, thinking I'd join the vendors in vests down by the river selling pocket art from their wagons, or sing with the women crooning ballads for a piece, or talk with the men with suitcases full of postcards on which I could write poems across and post to home, all or any of this down by the brown river that runs by us all, the brown river that can't capture everything that happens on its banks, but some, if just enough, of the quiet sampling, of each love, of each whisper, of each breath.

13

Of Cabaret

The half-moon seemed to drift, but it wasn't; it was just the appearance of the moon wandering about in the sky. I noticed this as I climbed from the car and looked up to the house on the hill where I could make out a small fire in the trees and the sounds of people lingering, huddling for warmth. We had come together under one moon and one sky to perform, to watch, to clap, to drink, to bark, to shout, to be free. I saw an exhibition and parade of adornment: a woman dressed as a bunny with ears, full bodice, petticoat, and large skirts layered over her curves and hips. A man as a coyote with ears on his head, a costume of fur about his torso. They sang a John Prine song and went playful on the stage flirting and making dreams come true. A kitty. A man goat. A mute flapper. A woman with the name of a fruit. A lesbian beauty who told jokes about being a gay parent, maybe an unfit one she joked, but not really; how lucky a kid to be the receiver of such an arrangement of love. Many tails, much glitter, tights, and a band who screamed guitars and "Crimson & Clover" to the stars with barrels of fire warming us and our cold breath in the air. A woman dressed as a tiger danced and growled under black light. Two women read sexy poetry and pretended to have the kind of sex you don't talk about—one with stuffed balls at her split of thighs, the other with a tight stretchy thing over her crotch. A naked man with tattoos and a sort-of mohawk read poetry from his journal. He had volumes of texts he could have read from all night. A bar served gin, but I brought wine and drank the whole bottle and could barely stand at one a.m. when the spectacle finally ended and a man with a top hat and sparkles on his face recited Dr. Seuss and oh, the places you will go, holding us rapt, while a girl with a ukulele who was cute with a flower in her hair strummed the strings and sang silly songs that made us all laugh. I had to duck under fishnet tights and women in wigs kissing in order to pee in the bathroom with clay walls. That night, I saw a sadness on some faces. Or maybe I was the one who was sad. An oak sculpture of a snarled snake hung from the ceiling above a red velvet couch on which were splayed people, drunk or high, and the band played in the dark cold and the music bounced off the trees and shook the animals in their hiding places. All I wanted to do was dance to the heavy guitars or kiss a man I didn't know, or at least, let one desire me, let one strip off my brown jacket in the woods behind the house, let the pine needles tangle in my hair, let the mushrooms stain my lace skirt even though it was cold, even though it was November, even though I was married, even though I'd get sick, I didn't care, he would strip my brown jacket, maybe pull up my shirt to the cold and fulfill that untouched place most men want to go, but can't, because there is no way a man can ever fully know what a woman holds inside her; it's so deep it burns even into the morning when the light has washed away all dreams, sins, impossibilities.

14

A Country Wedding

—Siskiyou Mariposa Lily, *Calochortus persistens*

We walked our rural road on a Saturday, the pavement saturated with the day's rain and littered with leaves shuffled from the trees at odds with the hardy west wind. Ava wore a brown dress speckled with white shapes like triangles, brown tights to match, and pink shoes. She was pretty with tiny braids wrapped atop her head, the rest of her auburn curls falling to the straight line above her hips. Everett held my hand, skipped along with his nice clothes and missing teeth lost now to the spaces in his grin like open doorways. As we walked, you told me of your dream: about a woman who took you to dinner, a woman not your wife, a woman not me. Your father disapproved of this, handed you cigarettes and said, "Smoke them or don't," and you laughed in the re-telling while we walked under the heavy sky with the sun splintering the day with so much clear light, strips of ribbon we could walk through on our way to the next farm over for a country wedding at the tip of autumn.

Funny how our dreams become laughter or story to fill our talk, our time together.

There were children everywhere in the wet grass when we arrived, and too, a pig roasting in a box, an arbor made of madrone branches, a band coiling wires. We said hello to our old neighbors and made acquaintance with the new. I eyed a young man in a floppy hat looking like something straight out of a hay pile. He asked me to dance, later, when you disappeared to the pie or trees where our son chased other boys down by the black creek. I can't lie—dancing with another man under the moon was dangerous and enchanting, so true in its simple shape of attraction, of desire, of want.

The officiant told a story. He said, "This story might be true, but it might not. I'm not concerned with the facts." He told of the Grand Canyon, the layers of rock compared to a marriage over time—the soft new love of the rudimentary bands to the deeper depths of rock where intimacy lives. I held your hand while the bride smiled in her sheen and silk dress of blue with an appliqué of branches and tree swirling around the hem and up through the bodice, a diamond brooch at the split of her breasts, and flowers in her hair, of course. The groom wore buckskin pants sewed at night in his cabin, his muscle and bone sliding into the leather so effortlessly like he was born into them. He was barefoot in the clover.

I drank too much hard cider brewed by the apple farmers up the road while the band played music that carried me away under the silver clouds shifting and mixing in the aftermath of the earlier storm. The string lights overhead cast a glow about the place that made every shadow count, illuminating the cheeks of all the people who sipped and talked and celebrated. The light made us all beautiful.

Later, we swayed back down our road way too late with that harvest moon peeking through the clouds and our children thought I was silly because I chattered on about the essay I was writing, a rejoinder to a rejoinder, and how we were to make an experiment with eggs in the morning. I rambled all this while I pushed them in the stroller, heavy with umbrellas, sweaters and pouches of lavender, party favors we could tuck under our pillows when we arrived home. They didn't understand my slur and stream of words and said, "Mamaaaaa," all drawn out and laughing. I wished for them to remember this laughing, this joy.

That's when the clouds parted and our field came into view, bare now after having been mowed that morning, and our farm looked as if it were a bowl, the beauty difficult to describe even, but I felt it pulling us toward it, this container of our life, and of many things, like love and work and someday, death. I saw the field washed in moon glow, fine and bright, and everything we keep was revealed to me as I tipped over sideways from the cider, the music, the marrying.

I think I'm writing this now so I'll remember what I feel about this place that holds so much for us. So I'll remember it wasn't just a dream we laughed about once when we were young and buoyant and drunk on mountain cider. I think I'm writing this for you. So you'll know.

15

Of Daughter

"There's a fly, a fly, a fly. There's a fly, a fly, a fly." And then, "I swam to the whole side of the pool. I did, to the end, to the end of the pool. I did. I swam to the other side." My daughter and her Seussian monologues. "If I eat all my dinner, I can have an orange. Dad said, I could have an orange. If I eat all my dinner. I'll have an orange." Over and over again, she sings her rhythms to me and I capture them. Write them down. It's the music I play for her. Her favorite song is the whine of a New Orleans banjo and the haunting voice of a swamp mistress singing tunes of the bayou. Or the musical influence becomes the string guitars and sad melodies I love to hear. I play this music for her so she talks to me in patterns that beat the air and I listen with attention to catch the suggestion of meter and pulse. I hope she'll be a dancer, an artist, maybe a singer. I hope she'll love herself more than I have. I hope she'll have many lovers. I know these longings are mine, not hers. She stares at me as deep as the earth and tunes out her words to the silent space between us, a distance now close but forever receding, hoping I will hear her, hoping I will acknowledge her voice.

16

Gather & Fetch, or the Narrator on Memories

My grandmother crafted shadowboxes and hung them on the wall in
her two-bedroom home, a one-story spread with a fine backyard
encased in broken fences. They were her own chimeras, daydreams
manifested, maybe all that she hoped for in her one small life, a
reconciliation of neglected dreams: were she to be a writer, an opera
singer, a woman who rode horses. Perhaps the shadowboxes were a
portrait of all that went unnamed at the end of a long era suffused with
raising children on food stamps and dirt, children who were now
adults with their own babies, their own neglected dreams, their own
failures and disappointments—divorce, alcohol, poverty, wealth. In her
boxes, I'd find little people with fabric dresses and yarned hair, all
with their little things—desks and chairs, wash bins, toilets, tea cups,
rolling pins, toasters, spatulas. Clocks and birds and spools of thread.
I wasn't allowed to touch them, though I did after she went to bed,
when I prowled her hallway, only a shimmer of light coming from the
family room. I took them down from their tiny shelves, shifted them
around in my hands, explored the detail of their artistry, and sought to
learn their meaning. I liked to rearrange them, shuffle their
placement, see how they might assemble themselves into new
positions. I handled them for as long as I thought, until the guilt of
disobeying my grandmother overcame me, so that I'd quickly replace

the little things back to their shelves. I never wanted to disappoint my grandmother, or worse, cause her to stop loving me. I wonder now if she knew their placement as well as she did the freckles on her arm, or the way the front door sounded when it shut. I scuttled in a rush from the dim hallway, always back to my guest room, the only thing left was the silence of a house asleep with a low buzz of television voices from the other room where my grandfather dozed to the late-night news. What story did she want to tell on those walls? Some sort of alternative narrative devoid of the terrible quiet issued forth by her rural life? Where quilting and mule races and warm soda and thin cigarettes were the afternoons of her marriage to the Owens Valley, to her husband, her sons, my father?

*

Every December, my mother gifted me Madame Alexander dolls. Over the years, the cardboard boxes gathered in precise stacks in my closet, preserved in perfection: cotton dresses with frilly aprons, plastic hair with glue, hands with fingers that could not move. Nothing about the dolls was real, the rosy cheeks that weren't brushed by wind, lips so red they looked as if they wore lipstick. They were only small, delicate things. I was never to play with them very long, if at all, but in defiance I pulled them from their boxes every so often when I was alone, just for a moment, when the house was quiet, and smoothed the skirts, adjusted the bows in their hair, fingered their soft saddle shoes. I lined them up on my bed and kept them there while I brushed my hair in the mirror, or wrote an entry in my diary, then one-by-one, I put them away into their blue boxes, shelved them and shut the closet door, the memory of them just as sure as my grandmother's shadowboxes hung in souvenir along the walls of her home.

*

A few memories from that time: the Safeway, always, and the sad people with coupons in their hands pushing carts filled with cereal and donuts. My grandmother's silk nightgown draped over my shoulders, creeping down over my feet, too big for a girl, but special in its silk and feel. I was a lady, adorned in a lost generation, my grandmother's grace a special kind of hand-me-down. Hot leather seats in a Buick waiting for fish sandwiches at the drive-thru window. The toy store, my grandmother's hands, the dolls lined up on shelves in pink boxes, an unknown story of hips and plastic eyelashes.

Yes, this is nostalgia. Heaps of it. So too, glasses clinking in the kitchen after that, when the adults mixed drinks at four. Stale smoke settling into my hair. Conversations I could never understand, strained and tensed to the window shades. Just as my own children now might stand in the kitchen wondering about my laughter, the voices of their mother, father, our drinks, the collected shelves of my books, or shoes, or dresses hanging unworn and spidery in the closet. Maybe they'd think to sip the melted ice from my glass after Josh and I have left the table for our argument in the next room, or maybe they'd go to the basement and draw out the photographs of deserts, and butterflies, and cousins in terry cloth shorts. Maybe they'd wonder about all that life gathered there between the cement walls dampened with summer dust. Maybe they'd find my grandmother's tea cup skimmed with porcelain purple roses. Perhaps they'd break the tea cup, crying the fragments into a bowl for us to piece together later.

*

I didn't know my grandfather except when he progressed into the garden for zucchini and corn or rinsed his black diesel hands in the sink. He didn't take me to the toy store. He didn't take me for French fries and hamburgers. I don't think he much spoke to me—even a word, a phrase, or something to say he knew I was his son's only daughter. I'd watch and that's how I knew him. He failed as a farmer as he failed at many things—a father, grandfather, husband. He tried to pioneer the country, in more ways than I could imagine—took cotton, oranges, and milk as his way, or at least tried. Never succeeding, his poor identity bound up with the junkyard of his rural home. He collected metal, tin, and rusty things in his garage and yard. His shed. Which is what farmers do. They store junk, piles of trash mostly, but tires, screws, these things having their importance, their place. I didn't know that then. With a hesitancy, a worry of intrusion, I explored the landscape of his world, confused by the layer of metal, the bolts, the tires, the fence. I wanted to sift through it all but didn't because I thought he'd scold me for touching the discarded pieces of his life. He tinkered, quietly, with a disinterest in the doings of the rest of the world. I watched as my father stood with him in the evenings, the day just a neatly laid cloth on the dirt of their hometown, my father's off-white slacks freshly pressed, saddle shoes clean and shining. He'd say, "What *is* all this out here?" looking around the piles, throwing his

hands around. My grandfather would mutter, "Well, let's see here . .
." and then he'd drift off, look out a bit into the sky, maybe squint,
watch the airplane cruising by at an altitude high and distant,
inconceivable. My father would wait awkwardly, a second or more,
look up at the sky too, then turn away, head back inside where the
women laughed, grab a cream cheese cracker from the plates of food
on the table, open another beer maybe, tasting the bitter cold liquid
while my grandfather stood alone in the hazy gray light of dusk, dirty
old hands brushing the space my father had just been standing.

*

I think about collected things—shadowboxes, metal, memories. How
we gather, accumulate, hoard, our basements or sheds filling with
boxes of objects. Or maybe we display these things, like I do with my
books, though it seems static, so burdensome to carry around things
we don't need. What is it all for? To give shape our desires. Like
Mozart's Don Giovanni. He collected sexual conquests. Henry
Wellcome, sharp objects. Soap bars, toaster ovens, penises from
mammals. Everett: plastic bags of cards, scissors, a watch, rope,
papers, homemade traps, thumbtacks, a whistle should he ever need
it. The more beautiful: William Sharp Macleay's collection of
butterflies, a stranger's assortment of old compasses lining walls I'll
never see. Susan Sontag wrote "to collect is to rescue things, valuable
things from neglect, from oblivion..." But I think, they rescue us,
become who we are.

*

There was a highway once, and it ran through a town dirty with litter and sweat and cars. This highway—paved with ambition—hastened like a quick shot between the line of shops and sidewalks, past the one stoplight blinking forever on by the Dairy Queen, beyond the last house on the right, and then slanted steep and up into the high desert mountains, heaving us out into meadows thick with flowers, wild and blue. This highway, I used to walk its burning shores, watch the heat take shape, consider the mirages that simmered up when it was so hot the mules couldn't even shoo the flies. Back in those days, in the town Bishop, I wandered down my grandmother's crescent lane under shady elms to the Safeway, and by the restaurants leaking smells of grease and burger, out to the north end of town where the trucks honked and the rabbit brush blazed. A place too far away now. A town almost mythic in its memory, lodged there for such a time, now evoking regret over fathers who drank, junkyards disguised in copper and tin, all the silent disagreements, sometimes laughter. Or perhaps it's nostalgia: the way we collect certain items of our youth and pack them into selected memories and images—Barbie dolls, horse races, backyard sprinklers, card sharks. But then too, it might be a remembered longing for a future not yet furnished, a story still to grow. This is all to say I lived among people who mined the world for meaning based on small things amassed. This is all to say this is how I remember them.

17

Of Love

Husband, you are a city I want to get lost in, where the roads always circle back and there's rain and frogs. A silver light in your hair. Fir trees and sheets. The hungry air between us. Your hands are urgent but I slow you. You tell me you are overwhelmed by my body, my skin, my hair. You kiss the fold of my pelvis, my thigh. I say, let's draw this out. But then something takes over: a pressing. No turning back now. The laundry needs folding. The fire in the stove has died. We forgot to put the cheese away. The dirty knife. Crumbs on the counter. Then it's over. I lie on my side. You rest your too strong hand on the curve of my hip. Just above. You tell me you are thinking of this spot on my body. I don't know what you mean, but it doesn't matter. I've told you I love the white hair that streaks into your beard just below your right ear. I think how I'll write this for you on Valentine's Day. I think, I'll undo this beauty by the end of the year. Sleep comes fast for you. The rain comes even faster. The frogs go quiet. Just the moon then. And breaths like smoke from chimneys. Above this city which you are.

18

For Today, or the Narrator on Living

Like anything—the finch, the tortoise, the coreopsis—we pass on, so then, what else but for today?

Let's take this simple: a game of mancala with the boy when the girl of my heart naps in dreams. I move plastic animals back and forth in a circle on the wooden board—pink elephants, green zebras, red goats, purple lions. Everett takes a bite of apple he shook from the tree and says, *The green, this is the livingly part, the part we live with. The red tint of the apple,* he says, *we leave that.* I ask, *Why* and he shrugs. I think, maybe for when we are desperate, for when hunger is nothing more than a thin ache, for when we need a little color.

I look up the word "livingly" in the dictionary. I think there are many ways to understand what he's made new in this speech. *Livingly*: a manner of living perhaps, livelihood, of being alive.

Later, I take a walk along the shore of a lake in an afternoon hot with heat, then stand in the outdoor shower, the grass tickling at my shins, or heels, and the sky, I see, through the slats in the wood, is an empty blue, so empty and wide it makes me lonely. The dog licks the grass and the children run above me on the deck, my worry the size of a skyscraper—that the children will fall through the railings, trip, or the dog will push them and I will be in mid-shampoo as Ava thuds to the ground and the beetles, they will take her first.

One afternoon, I run with the children, down the slope, and through the grass that has fallen over and cracked, bursting with too many spiders to stay alive, and there, I laugh with them in the grass, too dead for anything but hay and clippings. I think, scraping my hand on the hull of grain all around me, that someday, my mother will die. My children too. And how will I know what it feels like to become death? Will it be as the morning is every day, like how confusing it is for me to be in the same bed at the same hour but with the call of the scrub jay the first thing I hear? Is it like that? Will I lift the shade of my bedroom window on the day after my mother's death and still see the tree, the apple tree with its vast flowers and fruit still as beautiful as the day before?

19

Draw Two Circles, or the Narrator on Distance

In a boy's hands, a trumpet, played to the open window at an hour of seven. I can't tell you the particular bounce of the notes, or the technique used to craft the song, the scale, the high register of tune. All I know is the sound, the push of brass into the night, the wind of it really, that held me there on a narrow sidewalk in Vermont, a far stretch from my home, a place distanced, almost a memory. I noticed the artichokes, and the sky, of course, bursting into a stream of color in moods of the sun. I sipped my beer, a cold can of hops and grain, swatted the mosquitoes from my arms, pretended the boy with the trumpet could not see me lingering on the concrete, my sandals off and tossed to the side, the pavement still warm. I faked playing with my phone so he could not tell how I listened.

There's so much to be said about home: how the nest box sets on the fence and the swallows station on the power line, their triangular alignment over the comfrey and fescue, the orchard grass overrun with seed already. It's June and the orange poppy with plum veins running up the petal's skin unfolds to reveal a bud of stamens like a clenched fist, a little girl's tight heart. I walk around my yard, barefoot on the earth, watching for the thistles we don't weed. I have no boys with trumpets for neighbors, I have no song but the everyday sound—

wheels on gravel, children laughing, a tractor's distant rumble, the dog's last growl, altogether a chorus important and worthy of remembering.

During my visit, I returned to the trumpet house again and again over the coming days. It was the possibility of transformation that pulled me there, the chance to experience an incongruous placement in time, home and not home, and of the dissonance of this predicament, drawing toward something while also leaving it behind. We must become two selves at once in places we don't know, while we reach for that one thing, whether trumpet or garden, which holds us together. I think to know something of this pull and tug as well as the sound the trumpet boy made, the hesitation of the player as he learned his craft, the drawn-out tube of vibration, the hum, the buzz, the goddamned beauty of this funneled harmonic chrome: it's a consummation of melody I want to remember in times of dislocation.

Standing there listening the second time, I wished to abandon my things to the sidewalk, walk up the bricked path and settle into the rocking chair beneath the window that faces the street. Watch the birds. Sip. Rock. Listen while the children count up the field across the way with their soccer ball and youth, the house garden growing taller with dill, the fronds something like wild hair on strange people, and everything coming together into the pitch and slide of beat thrown by the boy inside, all brass, all high and low extension, all compensation to a fixed harmony and beauty of contrasts, that almost, just almost, cannot be named.

20

Ten Cents

—Western Scrubjay, *Aphelocoma californica*

When Ava swallows a dime, Josh tells me two days later with a casual, "Oh yeah, I forgot to mention." I look at him sitting on the couch in his cozy sweater, then to Ava standing next to me in her skirt and blouse, dinner's soup dried on her cheeks. I see she's okay and fine. I see nothing is wrong with her, but still, I shout, say, "This is irresponsible. Don't you think you should have said something? Does she need to go to the doctor? Have you checked her stool? I have to Google it."

*

I search websites for instructions on what to do, remembering where I was when the swallow happened: at a neighbor's house eating chicken soup, drinking cabernet from goblets, and arguing over first sentences. I remember I trusted Josh with the children that night. I remember kissing Ava before leaving.

*

Everett begins to cry because he made her do it, or at least he thinks he did. "I was tossing coins in the air," he begs. "She threw a dime and opened her mouth to catch it. I'm sorry," he says, cheeks a crush of pain, tears dotting his collar. The day wanes—the shift of light fading, and fading, then gone.

Ava cries too. "I didn't mean to," she whimpers, turning toward her bedroom with the tiny bed pushed up against the wall crowded with several wool blankets, plush toys, and discarded napkins. She shuffles away across the wood floor, returning just a few seconds later with more tears and a hot pink monkey wrapped around her shoulders.

*

The children continue to cry. It is so loud it feels as if the whole family is crying, all in a zoo of tears, but really, it is just the children filling the house with their sobs—an exponential echo in the small room where I argue with Josh. Josh sets his beer on the table, picks up the phone and calls immediate care while I continue to scream insults. I am aware I shouldn't scream; he's on the phone and not in front of the children (*Isn't this how you ruin children? Isn't this how you were ruined?*), but I do it anyway. I make him mad with my screaming, but it isn't until later I wished I hadn't.

*

Josh bundles Ava in her jacket (it's October, it's cold), Everett is wailing on the couch and I say, "Wait, I can take her in the morning. She's tired. It's not an emergency. You don't have to drive all the way into town. It's already been two days." Josh pauses in the entrance to the front door for what feels like a long time. He looks at me, singeing me with his fierce brown eyes. The expression on his face, his eyes, they tell me everything: after all my ranting, after everything I've shouted, he can't believe I've changed my mind.

*

He replies, "I can't stand to look at you." He takes her anyway. As he shuts the front door, I hear him cough and remember he's sick and tired and probably just wants to sleep, take something for the pain in his head, but I don't care. He can talk to the doctor.

*

The two of them leave in the car. I watch them from the dim light of my bedroom. Everett moans and hiccups, says, "What about Papa?" I touch his shoulder and say, "Let's watch a movie." There's nothing I can do about the argument now. I can't take it back. I can't call Josh on his phone. He won't answer. Looking out the window, I remember all the times he has driven away and I wonder if he'll come back as he always has, or is this the final departure?

*

I eat a bowl of soup. I make popcorn. I need a drink, so I open a bottle of hard cider, the strongest thing I have to drink in the whole house, but it's too sweet. I pour it down the sink.

*

I watch *Charlie Brown, You're a Good Man* and I can't believe it when Lucy tells Schroeder he'll have to give up piano when they get married so he can buy her sauce pans. I laugh because isn't it just perfect that of course, even then, in the cartoon, the girls are plotting against the boys?

*

Josh returns twenty minutes later. Ava didn't go to the doctor. "It was too far to go tonight," he says. "It's not an emergency," he reminds me. The dime is still in her stomach. She watches Charlie Brown with her brother and laughs when Snoopy sings.

*

The children won't go to sleep. Everett has a stomachache now. He goes to the bathroom four times, streaming diarrhea into the toilet so I make tea, tuck him into bed, put a warm compress on his abdomen, rub his forehead. I try to be his mother. I really do, but he spills tea all over my books, the table, the wall. I scold him so he cries hopelessly into his pajamas. Josh comes in from the other room to comfort him like some hero who knows what to do when Mama gets angry.

*

The children finally sleep, but in my bed, wrapped in down, side-by-side, curled up sweet and warm into the blankets because they wouldn't go into their own beds; everything has gone too far for them to be alone. Instead, they've drifted into hopeful dreams in the bed where we had conceived them.

*

I leave the bedroom and tell Josh, "I'm not sleeping with them. I want to sleep on the couch. Just so you know." Josh throws his bowl on the floor. Rages out the door. I want to apologize when he comes back, but he won't let me. I press him and he says horrible things. I can't even write them here now; it would be too much. He threatens to leave me, grabs my laptop, promises to break it in half, but it doesn't matter if he ruins it. He can break everything I own and it won't hurt me. The hurt is already done. I retreat to the stool in the bathroom in the dark and hide while he explodes around the house. He reminds me of my father and the way he used to fight with my mother. This scares me, but soon enough, he's gone out into the night somewhere he knows I won't go. It's only later I find out he was in the car. It's only later he says to me, *You're going to fucking write about this, aren't you?*

*

I slip into bed with the children. I need them now, but I don't sleep. I turn the lamp on. I read, but can't. At three a.m., I hear Josh come inside and settle onto the couch. I leave the light on and maybe I sleep. I don't remember.

*

He leaves early in the morning before sunrise. I don't rise to say goodbye. After breakfast, I check Ava's stool in the toilet with a plastic spoon. There is no dime and Google says not to worry, so I send the children to my in-laws' house for a sleepover. I tell them about the dime. I don't tell them about the fight. I spend the day staring out the window and at the pretty tree with the yellow leaves.

*

I look at websites too, about marriage and fights and divorce, read *Dear Sugar* columns. Nothing helps. I know he is wrong. I know I am wrong, but I'm tired and sleepless and how do I repair the mess I made? I read things on the Internet like "Some men have no clue how you feel" or "Leave him, I would" or "This is how you know your marriage is over." I think—these quotidian concerns, the insignificant conflict of a dime—these could undo my marriage.

*

I leave at dusk. Josh is still not home. I go to a benefit auction and dinner alone, the date I was supposed to go on with him, so I drink too much red wine, barely eat the fish on my plate, tell my friends the horrible things he said, question whether I should even tell them. They are shocked and hug me. Pat me on the shoulder. I am thinking it's over. I am thinking he won't want me anymore. I go outside and cry, send Josh a text, tell him I am not coming home. He shouldn't worry if he doesn't hear my car. I apologize and wish for an answer. Something. Anything. He never replies. He is ignoring me, so I spend too much money on an ugly table and don't care if anyone thinks I'm drunk.

*

I go to a party after the auction. I smoke, drink, and talk to a ten-year-old boy whose aunt has forgotten him. I think I could do well by going home with another man. I fantasize about it. I think I could do this because a man I like says I am smart and beautiful and when he tells this to me, I think about Josh who may never forgive me, who may never want me again, who is at home asleep on the couch right now. I really want to believe I could go home with this man because I am swirling in the haze of the night with so much red wine and now pot that someone mixed into my hand-rolled cigarette and soon I am on the porch in the night with this smart and beautiful man eating popcorn and discussing pot farms. He stretches his arms above his head as if he's ready to go and says to me, "It's late. I'm tired. Do you need a ride?" I shake my head no. Many times, I shake my head no.

*

I go inside and talk with strangers about public forests, endangered fishers, old growth trees. Someone calls me wholesome and I think that's funny because that's not what I am and never have been, but this person doesn't know my history. This person thinks I'm sweet. Nice. A farm girl. I turn from him to watch women in the living room fondling and smoothing each other to music that's too loud, and I wonder what they will do or how far they will go. I'm fascinated with the women; I watch them for a long time until they notice me staring, so I wander into the kitchen to find a friend talking to a man I don't know, have never met. He's skinny and crying to her about the borders between Mexico and the United States, government corruption, Latino workers and what is happening to everybody? I'm not sure, so I shrug my shoulders, eat more popcorn, listen to pop music on the radio.

*

Someone burns a toy zebra in the street. They look for an accelerant, but it doesn't need one and the fire strips the toy to metal and I say, "It looks lonely." Its finish, its demise, its loneliness is like mine.

*

I sleep at a friend's house on her daughter's bed because I can't drive home and it is strange not to have Josh next to me; his absence is so large I feel it in my chest, my stomach, my throat, everywhere. I can't sleep because I have drunk too much, so I look around the room at the girl's lip gloss, lotions, hairspray while I lie there wondering why Josh never cared to check on me. I think maybe I should have slept with the smart and beautiful man precisely because of this disregard, the uncaring silence (*and what about Ava with the dime, is she okay?*), but then I wake after a few hours of bleary sleep and I am happy I didn't leave with the other man—the regret would be too much, the repercussions too great, but still, I don't go home.

*

I eat breakfast at a cafe with my friend. She tells me what to do. "I think Ava will be fine. My son swallowed a penny once," she says. I nod. "I also think your marriage will be okay. This is just a passing fight." I nod again. I agree to go home after finishing the eggs, the bacon, the toast, the oranges. I agree to let the dime go.

*

Later that afternoon, I return home to my quiet husband who won't look at me. The children jump into my lap, demand that I read to them. Soon enough, my friend sends a picture to my phone of the burned zebra in the middle of the street and writes that its ruined frame reveals the essence of the zebra and I think it is lonely still, and sad and unwanted, and I consider going to her house and taking it home so I might place it in my yard as a reminder of all the things I can lose over something as simple as a dime.

21

Pirate Radio, Like Desire

—Red Fox, *Vulpes vulpes*

I used to think being a pirate radio DJ was important, that this made me special in some way: a dissident, a rebel, subversive. I considered pirate radio a resistance to conventional life, whatever the prevalent notion of the ordinary. Though I have an inclination to denigrate my tiny world, subject it to insignificance, disruption from the customary carries gravity and surprise. Like here. But ultimately, I was avoiding sameness.

The station—a sixteen-foot trailer on wheels with poor ventilation and flat tires—was located in the trees on a spread of land shared with a pre-school and playground, a garden and swing set, next to a cannabis farm and cattle ranch, surrounded by public land and second growth timber cuts.

It was there—at the station, on the land, by the school, next to the cows—I met the radio man. M_ played hip hop at midnight on a Tuesday, lived in a cabin in the high mountains, bookshelves lined with Noam Chomsky, Chuck Palahniuk, Derrick Jensen. His fence was broken, but you could see the stars just fine.

It all started when I was late into a night of drinking with a beautiful friend, S_, whom I secretly desired (broad shoulders, six feet in height, hikers' calves and hands with many lines)—the stars thin, the October night very cold. We smoked joints and drank beer while he listed off *Free Will Radio*'s diversity of shows—Americana, Heavy Metal, Bluegrass, Hip Hop, Dr. Science on Wednesdays. He said, "You should do it. You'd be good." Ever since I was a small child, I've searched for the bolder experience, craved the contemporary sophistication. I've never held a job for more than five years. I read obsessively for want of knowledge. It is difficult for me to sit through a film, even a very good one. I become distracted easily when something new comes along. And too, I like to be noticed and this collective of anarchist men running an illegal station in the woods was just the distraction I craved. I knew I'd be great at this endeavor: wooing listeners with Bikini Kill rioting on the airwaves, talking stories on air, drinking red wine from mason jars. I am also easily flattered.

My show aired on Sunday nights, so when the sun dipped behind the mountains, when a cast of shadows appeared on the driveway like a collection of actors ready to play out a scene, I drove my diesel truck to the station to play music to the few who listened: some on the frequency, some tuned in through the online streaming application— maybe several, or ten, twenty listeners. I liked listeners, of course— they mattered to me—and over time, my audience grew, but what mattered entirely, which was so utterly important to me, was that *Free Will Radio* was free.

It didn't take but a week for me to design a show: *The Knotty Edge*, a mix of indie, punk, neo-soul and electro-pop—Cat Power, Shakey Graves, Sylvan Esso, Karen O—with a bit of story and poetry thrown in as accessory entertainment. Even now, I still return to the same mixes as a way through memory. To remember.

Pirate radio breaks genre, moves out to new ground, making tracks in the woods like a fox. Pirate radio is a middle finger at the institution of radio.

No one knew where the station was located, just a few trusted friends who wouldn't leak the secret, though I brought my children there before school and let them wear the headphones and move the buttons on the soundboard. I never told them not to tell. *Free Will Radio* remained nebulous, hidden, something to intrigue and discover, echoing a register and chronicle of low bass and lyricism stretched out between the stars.

I brought M_ beer to his radio show. I left him music on a flash drive. I sent him emails faking questions so he might talk to me. I gave him my number. I flirted with him at the local taco shop while Josh drank beer across the room and managed our children's chaos.

On my show, I said and did what I wanted, except for three rules: I could never talk about anything political, I couldn't curse before ten p.m., and the geographical location could never be disclosed. But even those rules were regularly broken. I often forgot and said "fuck" on the air, usually right after I started at eight.

To woo M_, I brought him a book of hip-hop poetry from the Nuyoricans, lines and rhymes I thought might capture his attention, with a note signed with my DJ name, *Mazzy Maple*. I didn't know him, had only listened to his show and heard him talk about Kurt Vonnegut and play soulful hip-hop like nothing I'd heard before: J Dilla and D'Angelo, Talib Kweli, Erykah Badu. I thought maybe he was a poet.

While at the local store buying a six-pack with Ava in tow, the school bus racing by out the window scraping the highway toward homes and dinners, a friend stopped me. "I heard you last night on the dial. I loved that one tune. The one with the fiddle. And the Kills too. So good!" Sometimes in the school yard picking up Ava: "I was driving home last night and heard you playing Patti Smith. Turned it up loud!" Or I'd receive a message on Facebook: "I just have to write and tell you how much I love your radio show. I discovered so much new music within a half-hour. Thank you!" I was my own local radio star, which stroked my ego and fueled love for fame. David Bowie crooned, "Fame, it's not your brain, it's just the flame that burns your change to keep you insane." Always I want to be seen. Always to burn. If only to heed Virginia Woolf's advice to "go on adventuring, changing, opening my mind and my eyes, refusing to be stamped and stereotyped. The thing is to free one's self: to let it find its dimensions, not be impeded."

How to explain the ways radio filled me: the nuance of desire, of waves and vibration, both sound and longing, the need to create a charge of want, to stretch heat and flush over the surge of radio. How when I though or knew M_ was listening, there was nothing else. How when I played, I shuddered with nerve and pleasure and all thrill. Music was the in-between filling the spaces before we met, before touch. A conduit.

A friend designed a seasonal radio flyer for me to reflect the change in mood and temperature. The posters were seductive with pictures of women and lips and headphones, something to evoke Nina Simone singing the *Gin House Blues* with her head wrapped in a scarf and a cigarette on the piano. I liked to tell stories with my Facebook posts accompanied by pictures of Joan Jett, Deborah Harry, microphones, hearts streaming chords, women smoking bongs, old ladies dancing to rock 'n roll, or memes that declared: "Warning: Punk music may cause creativity." Sometimes, I'd theme a show: *Because I'm feeling edgy and because the influence of the Aries new moon has everyone fired up, tonight's The Knotty Edge is all blues, all rock, all guitars,* posted with a picture of the Black Keys looking cool and mean in black and white. Or: *I'm celebrating Easter with beer, Twizzlers, and Nina Simone among others.* I thought about the descriptions the week before my show, thinking how I might impress, how I'd arrange the music, how I'd entice people to listen. I suppose it was a puzzle for recognition.

Something then about breaking rules. Fragments, which are sentences and not sentences. "Note: the passive voice has often been criticized as something employed by people in power to avoid responsibility." I must be a liability then, to literature, and radio, probably both, and maybe marriage too.

"It is important to start by recognizing the truth about pirate radio stations. They are not cute; they are not filling a niche; they are not innovation test beds; and they are not training grounds for future broadcasters."—Michael O'Rielly, FCC Commissioner, April 8, 2015

Victor Hugo wrote, "Music expresses that which cannot be put into words and that which cannot remain silent." Discover that tonight on The Knotty Edge as I play another beautiful mix of new music and old favorites at 8:00 until 10:30 p.m. on www.freewillradio.org. Stream live every Sunday night. #communityradio

Fake turf carpet covered the ground in front of the station to soak up the rain and to provide a certain backwoods aesthetic, or maybe it was meant to be ironic. We pitched an old coffee can to the side for cigarette butts. There was one folding chair, a tarp for an overhang. The trailer itself was surrounded by a circle of fir and madrone, the neighbor's field an expanse of hay and seed. Inside, posters covered the ceiling—Prince splayed in some stretchy, spandex thing. Bumper stickers glued to the walls: *Fuck the police, Fire to the prisons.* The *History of Rock N Roll* sat moldy on the speaker. Someone hung a framed cross-stitch of a kitten mewing for attention and the front window had broken long ago. Even with duct tape, still, cold air came in. No one bothered to fix it. It was small in there, tight, cozy, with a bar chair and cushions for the benches, a space heater or fan, depending on the season. Compartments above held bongs, tobacco, lighters, weed, toilet paper. Beer cans littered the floor and benches. The air contained a kind of stale smoke quality mixed with sweat and beer.

I was breaking new terrain by exploring the fragile and dangerous strand of want. I wanted anarchy in identity. I wanted everything that I wasn't already. I wanted to upset that comfortable notion of home and head straight into longing.

I sent **M_** an email asking him out for a drink. I gave him my number. He texted me not too long after, which began the flirtation. "Enjoyed your couch story last night. It was poetry. Keep 'em comin'. Maybe this weekend we can go out for a drink. Happy genocidal maniac day!" We did this back and forth for many weeks. He'd listen to me and text me. I'd listen to him and text him. "Awesome show last night! Thanks for playing my requests. Hope you recover from Ebola soon so we can go out."

With Venus, Jupiter, and the Sun all meeting in Leo and a moon on the wane, this week's The Knotty Edge will indulge and inspire your wildest passions, so pour yourself a sweet or spicy glass and drift with me into a dreamy, bold, and extravagant collection of melody and song tonight at www.freewillradio.org.

The act of collage is to mix, to create a juxtaposition of images, threads, space. Answers don't come easily in collage; they must be searched for, explored. DJing is a collage, as in the order and arrangement of songs. The nature is incomplete, the evolution of truth apparent and clear only toward the finishing, the absolute. Collage as a combination of texture, style, beat, rhythm.

At the station, I had no boss. I didn't get paid. Nobody told me what I should or shouldn't do. It was the essence of prerogative.

In any art form, there's a relationship between the artist and the participant—a theater goer, a reader, an art collector. In radio, it's the listener. The means in-between is the microphone. So comes the DJ's voice, the invisible listeners, a relationship of loyalty and faith. Of trust. A radio show—composed, organized, delivered—with beauty and craft draws it close, sews itself to the form.

"Everyone has the right to freedom of opinion and expression; this right includes the freedom to hold opinions without interference and to seek, receive and impart information and ideas through any media and regardless of frontiers."—Article 19, the Universal Declaration of Human Rights

This desire to create both art and love was an inquiry into the influence of attraction. For many months, M_ and I listened to the other over the radio, creating art and desire in collaboration. We were a new art form, wild with frequency, pulsing with high beat and emotion. I'd play a song and he'd send me a brief text, "Nice choice." Or he'd comment on my Facebook post, "Yea! Good show!" I sent M_ requests that informed him of my sentiments. He'd promote me on his own show, "Check out the Knotty Edge on Tuesday with Mazzy Maple. Always good music." A subtle magnetism, so created to become permeable, two people banded on the same spectrum, tuned and listening. Or maybe I wanted to believe it was something more than it was. I chased him as a lion to a mouse.

"After silence, that which comes nearest to expressing the inexpressible is music."-Aldous Huxley. Listen to the inexpressible tonight on The Knotty Edge. Feel the vibration at 8 to 10:30 pm, PST. Stream live at www.freewillradio.org #communityradio

The Radio Act of 1912, under President Taft, ordered that unlicensed radio transmissions would be illegal, as a response to the sinking of the Titanic, though radio had nothing to do with the ship's accident. When transmissions from amateurs interrupted the navy's own broadcasts, regulation followed. At first, amateurs created their own frequencies, and Taft allowed illicit broadcasts, but eventually, the FCC formed and licensing was required.

Eventually, I grew serious at pairing songs and melodies that told a story I wanted M_ to hear alone. This was my own story I created for him, though I still wonder if he ever knew. I wanted him to know. I wanted him to be intuitive and understand the message I was sending.

Pirate radio is an opposition to the standard. It stands up for what it wants as an act of defiance. This can make for influence, as leading in thought. It's becomes a place where art transforms, if so delivered with impulse. It leads with resistance to narrative, to structure, or an upholding of structure in new imaginative realities. An arc of story consumed with the music of nature, of vision.

He joined me on my one-year anniversary show and after three hours of whiskey and talk of buffalo and cats, I kissed him on the turf grass. He didn't hesitate, leaping at the chance to touch me. It was as if he had been waiting all this time. It could have been too easy to lay down right there in the dark under the stars, though I knew Josh was listening alone at home, our children asleep in the next room. I let the music roll on the dial. We stopped after too long, knowing we couldn't go farther.

In 1958, Radio Marcur, the first "pirate radio" station, broadcasted from Denmark on a vessel traveling through international waters without a license until 1962 when the Danish parliament disrupted the programming.

To be desired was to become something bigger than myself. M_'s want of me, sexually and emotionally, defined a new identity: I was sexual, a charge of eroticism, beyond mother, beyond anything but the experience of the physical.

I loved my black Queen t-shirt and I loved to wear it just for M_. Partly see-through, he could make out the black outline of my bra through the cotton fabric. It spelled out, "I'm punk enough for you." It spelled out, "I can be what you want me to be."

Tonight on The Knotty Edge: Desire in all of its manifestations. *Music tonight will circle around longing, yearning, wanting and all those impulses, wishes, cravings we have as human beings. New music from Slow Club, Escondido, Shakey Graves, and others. Stream live at www.freewillradio.org from 8PM to 10:30 PM PST.*

There is a parallel expression of feeling in both music and movement that shifts and transforms. Music has the ability to evoke both physical movement and emotional "movement." Music as yearning. As desire. Radio as yearning. Movement as yearning.

Our collective of DJs pooled our resources together twice a year to raise money to keep the power on, the Internet streaming, and pay rent on the land from which we broadcasted. We had very little money, though the wealth that did come to us was often donated from marijuana growers' store of cash from the harvest in October. Our Free Will Radio costume party was a standard community event that earned a thousand dollars for the station and kept us streaming for six more months. The costumes became an oddity, a parade of fringe: the Ebola virus, a sexy sailor, a punk vampire, and on. Everyone talked about it for months.

I didn't feel anything but the need to be fulfilled by M_. I thought of Josh, yes, I did, but I couldn't stop. I had to keep going. I needed to know what it felt like to sleep with another man. I couldn't see the damage I would eventually cause. It was the transgression I desired. To be disobedient. To wander into unconventional terrain. I didn't want to be good.

It was all about mood, intimacy. That's why people listened regularly. There were no limits to what we could do. It was special, this ambience in which a listener and DJ interacted—a deep tenor among people, shared across an art form. When I played music, I wanted people to think a coyote was on the roof of their home, shouting out syllables, making sounds they'd never before heard.

Lyric: of music, of poetry, of emotion. I'm whispering in your ear. Do you hear me? It's after dark and there are things I want to tell you that nobody knows. Like secrets.

I think of my privilege often—to produce art, to write, play music. To seek desire from a man. To contain a level of freedom of expression and impulse unavailable to others. As the famous anarchist, Peter Kropotkin, wrote, "It is in the ardent revolutionist to whom the joys of art, of science, even of family life, seem bitter, so long as they cannot be shared by all." I'm not much of an anarchist if I can't taste the grievous. So maybe, pirate radio and desire as my own insurgence.

Dim the lights & break out the vanilla spice candles because it's all slow jams tonight on the Knotty Edge. Music by Denitia and Sene, Lily M, Marian Hill, THEESatisfaction, Prince, Hiatus Kiayote & more. Turning up the heat at 8:00 until 10:30 p.m. PST on Free Will Radio. Streaming live at www.freewillradio.org.

Jonathan Kramer, an American composer, said it's the attitude of the music that makes it postmodern. We broke commercial radio rules, playing what's not played, raiding the airwaves illegally. Locals knew where to find us and they knew what they'd find: raw radio, partisan with no advertisers. We reconstructed a new radio genre in reaction to rules and boundaries, dissent a model for expression, a pushback against elitism. Few rural stations play anything but cowboy music and

Britney Spears, but how loud could I go with the Ramones or the Misfits? What could Sharon Van Etten sing to the woods?

At a party, weeks after our texting and listening and kissing at the station, M_ and I danced close, and hot, to electronic beats. In the woods at the house of another DJ, we smoked cigarette butts from the trays outside and pumped the keg with our hands. It was October. I stayed out past four a.m. I slept all day, my children erupting onto my bed in the afternoon, my makeup smeared across my face, remembrances of his embrace and hands all over my body.

Desire as possibility, as opening for experience.

One night he took me to a house lit up with blue lights and a woman laid on the deck out back singing to the sky like some wild creature loose on champagne, or other ecstatic drug I didn't know. He pushed me against the deck railing, and we went like that for awhile.

Part Two: Break

"Both security and freedom are acts of the imagination. Neither of them are fundamental realities."—Stephen Mitchell

"Against enkindled desire, honour itself was feeble."—Virgil

22

Of Marriage

Josh tried to go along with my plan for an open marriage. He was
excited by C_. I was excited by M_. He willingly let me see M_ at the
radio station. He told me which type of six-pack I should take. I asked
him how I looked. I wore cut-offs, a flowery shirt that showed off my
breasts and waist, and a blue-button down long sleeve. Josh liked it.
Josh said M_ would love it. I could barely breathe driving to the
station: who the hell was I to be leaving home on a school night to see
another man, someone I hardly knew? Later, when it became serious,
and I wouldn't stop seeing M_, Josh became mean. When C_ didn't
like the open marriage arrangement and she never replied to Josh's
texts, Josh called me a slut. He never apologized. He sneered at me
when I'd go out. The trust of our agreement eroded. He worked
longer. I stayed out later. Later on, I'd get a tattoo on my forearm on
my birthday and he'd shrug and say, "Well, now you have *that*."
When we were separated, Josh slept with me in our farm trailer while
the children watched a movie in the house and then told me to go
home still lying there naked, comparing me to K_, a woman who had
finally reciprocated his advances. I could see it in his eyes, how the
shape of my body didn't compare. He crafted online dating profiles.
He told me I was a stupid feminist, that he didn't believe in my work
as a writer. I wanted him to understand how he'd abandoned me for

so many years: left me for his work, for the farm, for his determination and ambition. What is complicity, but collaboration and responsibility. A willingness. Contribution.

23

Ten Ways to Leave

—Manzanita, *Arctostaphylos uva-ursi*

I. She could go out the back door and down through the yard marked about in roses with hips and the overgrown grass, the juniper slope, the limestone soil and past the jungle gym where the children play out their dreams of kings and queens and kingdoms ruled with swords, fire, dragons, and sometimes happy endings.

II. She hears a story one afternoon and can't forget the image of a woman walking the highway at night, alone, having left her husband standing in the parking lot of a store where he has chosen smoke instead of love and so she thinks she could leave with that same kind of drama: treading the turnpike while he watches her from a convenient store window, the road spread out before her like a long strung-out piece of thread that will unravel the more you fuss with it, the more you tear at it with your fingers.

III. She could go while he is sleeping, but she thinks that would be unfair and doesn't he deserve just a little bit of reason? If she did leave that way, she could sit on the bed first, the children sleeping in the other room, and watch his chest swell to the night, put her hand on his mouth, see every part of him move in dreams or nightmares, something she's never done, never even been curious about, which makes her wonder. So maybe when the ice thaws, she'll sneak from the bed tiptoeing through the house to the door and exit into a landscape of disquiet, apprehensive of the choice to go, but surely confident in the fantasy she holds in her mind.

IV. She left him once for Montana, driving up the north highway and over the mountains into the snow, and that was it. She lived alone in a new place and she thought this was life chosen well, but she missed him, remembering when they drank beer on porches while watching cars and bicycles and stars heavy with sky. She talked to her sheets at night, grabbing the pillow for his absence.

V. Maybe they could go for a hike, climb to the top of a mountain and look out from there, the way they did with their children once, the spread of all that grass and rock and peak, the wildflowers a new thing. They ate lunch: cheese, chocolate, salami, crackers. On top of that mountain, the wind picked up and it blew their children's hair and they pointed to their house in its blue painted wood, just over the three ridges to the west where they could barely make out its slant and hold in the distance. They picked ticks from their hair because they lay in the grass laughing at the sky and it was spring, remember? Yes, she thinks they could go for a hike and she could leave him there with the children on the mountain. She could remember him cutting cheese into slices on his knee, listening for any movement in the manzanita.

VI. Or maybe that's too dramatic. Maybe they should just be straight about it—sit on the couch together over coffee, or more likely, a drink: bourbon, ginger, bitters, a little lemon, the kind she always makes for him in a small glass with ice. She might sit with him and look out the window and over all they've done together, everything they've created, and still know it is all lost to the past anyway. Maybe she would cry. Maybe he would too. Or maybe there'd be no tears. Maybe they would have used up everything they had in the build-up to that moment, so to some extent, the fatigue of a relationship would overcome them and they would be quiet in their chairs in that room when the shadows take over the floors and the walls and all they'd hear is the empty burden of what is absolute: the love having gone a long time ago slipped from them when they weren't paying attention.

VII. She could remember how they never did take a real honeymoon. She could remember how they watched a sunset over the water in Baja one time when they thought they knew love. She could go like a butterfly. Or the coyote they saw in a field, trotting in from a distance and surely the postman would stop in his wagon if he came along. They watched from the car, the animal poised in dangerous pursuit of its prey, all of it in the last flicker of day until the coyote ran up into the frustrated hills without dinner, without anything to take his hunger away.

VIII. Or she could remember how they left Homer's tomb one morning in Greece, the Aegean spread out behind them like a blue map made up of what they couldn't know. She could remember how they brushed their teeth on his grave. She could remember how they spit. She could remember how they held hands. She guesses that staying is a probability because of these memories, that story, those moments. She considers their weighted history over and over again and really, she thinks the complicated details of leaving are the only things that keep her there still. It's the mechanics, she'll say.

IX. She thinks about the train she once took through France, through Switzerland, through Spain. She rode the early rail and left him in Brussels, though she lingered in the entry to the hostel before she left, sat down on the couch, pulled him to her, let his head fall into her lap, their cheeks flushed from pints of beer. He walked her to the station through a storm and when he left, she sat on the depot floor wishing for coffee and one last night next to him in bed naked and in love. She can't recall that feeling now. She can't conjure it in this tired, cold place of leaving.

X. She could leave by writing the departure. Maybe that's the best way. There could be any number of scenes: stomping out of the restaurant throwing her napkin on the floor; sneaking out through the window too late when another man waits in an idling car; running away as if in pursuit chased by children or thieves or. . . ; in the car early in the morning with just the sprinklers and newspaper man; or a surprise retreat when he returns from an errand, the house packed up, or just her things packed up, the door slightly ajar, her coat waiting on the couch, hands fumbling with the zipper of her sweater or earrings and she thinks perhaps this is the most obvious choice, the most conventional and unoriginal of all departures, the one and only way she can retreat and leave behind the safest thing she's ever had, this story that was never supposed to end in this way, at this point, in this now.

24

Of Desire, Again

I didn't dare look too long: all that fine sculpture of his face, the auburn hair cut straight and short, just a dash above his eyebrows and eyes, blue I remember. I averted my eyes to the shopping cart, to Ava dancing around on the linoleum, to anywhere but his too handsome face and eager mouth. In the glow of such unfavorable grocery store light, I must have looked frizzy. He said, "You are my Sunday night fling," of course, in reference to my radio show he listened to on Sunday nights after his children were asleep. The wild blush of pink spread over my cheeks like a slow spill of ink. *Was I being coy?* I could tell he wanted to linger with me if only because of the soft innuendo of his gestures and his compliment, so open and endearing among the toothpaste and vanilla face cream. I couldn't hold back my awkward coloring with this gorgeous figure flattering me. I flutter even now recounting the interaction: the way he tipped his head in curious regard of me, the way his eyes penetrated—severe, but tender and subtle. I quivered at his closeness, taking off my coat and nervously laying it on top of my cart, watching his eyes move to my hip where Ava had pushed up my sweater exposing the pale winter skin. I folded the sweater back down pretending he didn't see, but he did, and at this, the blood vessels of my face swelled even more, pushing outward to the surface of my cheeks, the capillaries wider now, pinker, more pronounced with each minute that ticked. He continued on to ask about the music I played, the station, until Ava tipped over sideways to the floor, a result of her impatient tricks and silly balancing acts. "Mama, look at me," she begged. We smiled down at her as she danced her one-leg jig pushing boxes of accidental toothpaste to the floor in all her clumsiness. It was all so out of place there in the grocery store, with the music on the radio—I don't know which song— the buzzing of the yogurt refrigerator, and the lazy chatting of the grocery store clerks waiting patiently for us to pay. *Did we need eggs?* I couldn't remember. I didn't even have a list. I only knew I wanted to flee to the freezer section and hide with the peas and corn. Or run to the bathroom and check the mirror. But I lingered. He lingered. We were both married. We both had children. We'd only seen each other at parties. But for just that moment, in the grocery store beauty section with the shelves of coconut lotion and apricot lip gloss, we wanted to run away with each other and all it took was a little blush to say so.

25

On the Fatal Shore

—Douglas Fir, *Pseudotsuga menziesii*

I. {*mortality, or death*} Everett troubles himself to sleep each night he settles into bed, an occasion in which he worries his mind over death— his, mine, his father's. He comes to me where I stand in the kitchen fixing a nighttime snack, the day slowed to night, already unavailable, the windows open wide and yawned to summer. He whimpers like a hungry dog. "Mama," he says to me. "I can't sleep because of that thing. That same thing." I look down at him. "Death?" I ask. To be clear. So I understand. "What do I do?" he asks. I bend to kiss his face, the skin of his cheeks like the underbelly of some beautiful animal. I usher him back to his room, watch him climb the ladder to his bunk where he curls around his penguin, his moose, his elephant. They are supporting him too. "Dream good dreams," I tell him. He nods. I leave the room, and down the hall, I wonder about his pain, though I know he can't tell me all that he feels. I'll never be able to know the depth of his struggle. Or will I? How can we ever know another's interior? I wonder further: does he imagine his last moment of breath, perhaps something as a dark boundary, an edge he must stand on, a shore? Fatal somehow. Everett is a curious boy, dressing himself in shorts too big for his body, tying a piece of black rope around the waist to hold them up, but still, the trousers slip from his hips when he runs. He attaches to the rope a scabbard and pocket knife, a pair of scissors, a small flashlight, sometimes a compass, or key chain, whatever else he deems necessary and important. The buttons of his collared shirt are pinched into the wrong slots, gathering the shirt at his neck, which then creates an uneven hem, so much so that I glimpse his belly button through the plaid. His hair is wild brown, tussled and loopy, and he says, "I'm going to check the chickens, you know." He loves to work, be useful, to share in the chores of our home. He tells me this is the only way through his fear.

II. {*misfortune, or ruin*} It's about second chances. It's about love in the woods. It's about every passion. It's about sending your head down the river still singing the saddest love song ever written. Orpheus silenced the Sirens, caused bushes to bounce while he drifted about with his lyre, made the air spin with melody, charmed the squirrels, the fish. Orpheus traveled to the underworld, begged Hades to allow his wife, Eurydice, her life once more. He sang for her, wooed Hades with song. We know the story: Orpheus breaks the promise he makes to Hades as he ascends from the underworld with Eurydice following close behind. In a moment of obsession, anxiety, despair, worry, we can't ever know, Orpheus glances behind him and Eurydice disappears, their love forever gone, the second chance spilled to the wind, the passion of their symmetry buried in the dark. It's something like the boy's fear of never waking up to a new day, of never having the occasion to see the pale bounces of the morning's color shedding light onto his pillow, of never seeing his mother again, his father, the plumes of his hens.

III. {*important, decisively so*} When you hear "Fatal Shore" by Andrew Bird, it's the spareness of the song that strikes: the quiet beauty of such a tempo, a slow rise of bass, a few tender notes on the guitar. A small drum beat. Deliberate and measured. It's a song of grief. "When are you coming to shore?/To never fear anymore/fear anymore./Never know any doubt/know any doubt." Bird's voice assembles into a high pitch with just a hint of shakiness. The harmonies romance the listener, the back-up slightly higher than Bird, "Were you breathing it out/breathing it out." There's that bass down in the lows—a freedom to it all, a beauty that transcends the harmonies, a casual conversation of song, though the subject is death, the fear of our final moments. The A-minor chord, that's the one that strikes me in the gut. The undemanding bass, a few notes, the soul poured into and out of the melody. A simple "Aw sure." Andrew Bird, like Orpheus, can charm the wildest things, uproot trees, resurrect the story of his one true love. It's an uncomplicated song, but also, it's not: the slow turn of death, the search for that edge. It's what I want to hear at the end: something that makes the span of margins, of finishing, that less terrifying.

IV. {*inevitable*} Sometimes I feel like an idiot girl in one of Jane Austen's novels, swooning over a man, tripping over a branch so he might rescue me, notice me in the late afternoon light, touch the freckles on my nose, brush his hand over the closed lids of my blue eyes. As the real me, I'm searching the likes of such questions: *What does eye contact mean? Should I give him a gift? Why won't he talk to me? How do you know if he's into you?* Here's my fantasy and it's as much a part of the music as anything: I'd meet M_ at the radio station, our shared trailer with the crude soundboard, a tattered swivel chair, and an old microphone soon to crackle and break. Music like Bird's playing on the old stereo, the bass taking out the speakers, a distortion, a night just prime and absolute, a little breeze but nothing to make us cold. We'd drink together, beer or whiskey, dance beneath the pines, a little apart at first, then close and it would be the movement of our bodies, our eyes, the urgency of the moment all there was, the wanting exchange, the underworld just a possibility as if I could disappear from the trees, the embrace. Perhaps I could conjure the image of Simone de Beauvoir and she would sit with me in the woods, or in the radio trailer, inhaling smoke and laughing at the world and the many men and women we loved like it was all one big plan we'd laid out on a map of complex borders that, over time, would dissolve until there was nothing left at all.

V. {*concerned with fate*} Imagine two men playing chess on the street. One in a white shirt, the other in all black. The man in white had waited all afternoon for someone to play with him. When the man in black finally comes, they smoke, play, talk. They rarely make eye contact. It's all very leisurely. Consider the friendship that forms in just a span of minutes. Consider fate. I'm thinking of the trace of fatality: how it comes to us all, and the emptiness we feel because of it. That's what this is all about: seek the beauty, want the passion, hold the wild. I've imagined my own death and know I want to reach it like the downbeat of a song. I've watched my dog die on the kitchen floor, her eyes glassy, not full of terror, but open to whatever was to come. I don't ever want to see my son die. This: I want to type a lyric on the paper and hand it to the chess players so that they laugh as I stroll around the last corner, the bar's blinking red light open now for drinking.

26

Ever a Terrible Quiet, or the Narrator on Longing

I'll begin where the cues of heat and thrust of summer call up a list. I've made sangria in a desert storm, mixing wine and fruit and brandy into glass jars, passing the drinks around the back of a truck, spilling the liquor across my chest, my knees, making marks in the dirt the color of wine and earth. I've looked for turtles, scorpions in the desert, run down the hot face of a dune, the sand making a tune to the air, a buzz-like desert song. I've found pink flowers in cracks not wide at all. I've made love with a man, new to me, quickly, almost frantically, under a desert sky strewn with stars. I've gathered spines and stems of calico, primrose to garnish a table in the coming purple dark. It's here now: I mark out a register of transience, an unconscious/conscious recall of details with no defining storyline, just shards and slivers as in this index. Here, I'm tracing the Mojave, its devastating beauty, and the illusion of an empty landscape—dust, rock, brush, wide nothingness. So much of the desert—those fine soil crusts, elevated rain-shadows, translucent color—has fixed in my imagination all these years. I've made parts up, I think—segments of story existing now only as fantasy or invention.

*

On the last day of the year, 1999 to be exact, my friends and I took a wagon up into the hills above camp, our tents spread out on the sagebrush like we were bandits, though we had wine and mushrooms and condoms, no stolen goods from the city. We went to find the Burro Schmidt tunnel, what is/was a dark shaft of rock through the mountain, not even a mile long, just a hollow stretch of granite that took a man thirty-eight years to shovel out. We had a handbook of ghost towns, an ounce of marijuana, and plenty of rolling papers. The map said the road would be hard, maybe impassable. The book told us about the man—how he scraped out a hillside with picks and shovels, a four-pound hammer, dynamite, how he pushed through rock, silt, sand to make a thoroughfare to bring gold to the other side. At the time, I remember wanting the story of this man to be a certain way, like the tale of an outcast passing the time digging and scraping, on repeat like some chickadee chant, all just to push back the desolation of his desert home. I wanted his story to be one of loss, of love, of mourning, of vacancy, of despair. Maybe because I wanted to feel something he never did, or could, or he must have. His desire was something, if not everything. I wonder, when he came to the end of the tunnel, when light shot through the black and blinded him, did he think dark things?

*

Maybe it's a matter of scent like dirt and sage. That's how I remember. Another sensory cue. Or, of vision like the scrape of a wing across the seemingly black sky. In this, I'm trying to establish what the desert can or cannot do. I'm thinking about retrieving memory. I'm thinking about the brain, all pulses and synapses, a complex arrangement of cells that connect me back to the Mojave, thousands of feathery tips linked in unison and patterns that say to me: this is what happened.

*

On that trip, we came off the ocean from the west and dropped into the desert basin, the highway just a long pull into nothing and there, the Mojave presented itself as a secret, a broad collection of empty earth unusual for taking cover, though you can hide from danger, pursuit, or even heartbreak. You can pack away those things you don't want anyone to know. You can find a place not to be found. There was, and is, mystery in this place where things go unspoken, unheard, undiscovered, even at the split of day when the sun can show out the sand and the hawk and the skin of a hand—red and dry and cracked. I mean to say that no one goes there, so you can't be found. It's too big. It's too empty. It's too open.

*

I recall the Mojave now, a roll of basin and range, an expanse of valley so plain yet complex, layered with salt pans, saline lakes, dunes, boulders, yucca, and desert rose all pushing up against the boundaries of the Tehachapi. The Mojave in December: not finely lined and mapped like a geometric city, but rougher, less sharp in its edges and devoid of lights but for those hushed stars above. Quiet too, except for some subtle movement—the coyotes, a few rattlers in the sand or maybe a lonely jackrabbit burrowing in for the night. If there is wind, it blows in subdued until a storm passes through. Then you can't see for the particulate in your eyes. All you can do is close yourself, hope for relief.

Going up the vertiginous mountain, we smoked joints out the open windows to a flat sky with nothing but distance, the scent of cannabis filling the car and swirling out to the mesquite and juniper. The road was but a washed-out creek bed, all bumps and jolts and ruts. I can't tell you how high we were. I can't tell you because the pot created an atmosphere of hallucination, but too, something else beyond that. The heat, the dust, the deserted road, our two dogs panting in the back, the drugs—these sharpened our awareness in a way that makes all of life clear in the present tense. As our eyes blurred the road and our blood pumped quickly through our veins, our hearts brimmed with desert and sand, our focus shifting to whatever we came upon: a rock, cactus, snakes moving over the ground, scorpions, a fly, the sun. We lived in a cloud of our own time. I want to say nothing mattered—that place in time we all find ourselves at some point in our lives, when the world is what it is, with no consciousness of the past, no headway into the future.

*

Before too long—had it been hours? No one remembers—we found ourselves on top of the scrubby Copper Mountain, the desert spread out behind us like a great sea of brush. The heat, like an oppressive blanket, settled into each crack of skin. We parked before a cabin looking to fall over from age. A junkyard of rusted trash sprawled in every direction with just a few mice scuttling about. Maybe a crow. No sound. A woman emerged from the cabin, ninety maybe, in all of her wrinkled skin, wrapped in a housedress with hair a bird's nest of unbrushed gray. Our friend went to meet her. We saw the tunnel just behind the old cabin. We pointed. "There it is," we said.

*

This woman was like a part of the desert, venerable and hollow as she kinked her small head toward our friend. He told us later, "She whispered to me about her house and the things she kept. She pointed them out." He led her to the cabin (she was half-blind), a door through which we could not see, and we watched from the car, stoned and out of our minds with the desert, the heat, the absolute loneliness of the place. Where was he going and would he be coming back? He said, "The walls were papered with cereal boxes." Stacks of newspaper covered the floors. Ashtrays and every type of tin and copper piled about the tables. I think now there were motorcycles off in the mountains distant, their echo swallowing the dirt where we sat. I looked out the window, to the sky, past the cabin to the tunnel and hilltop, where a shatter of heat collapsed the air creating a mirage in line with my hazy mind, all of the heat intensifying the sweep of afternoon, a ghostly day, imagined maybe, a delusion even.

*

I can't remember walking the tunnel now. I want to say I felt the walls of rock cool underneath my fingertips, that I feared the dark, that I wasn't sure where we were going, what would happen. I want to say I couldn't see the other side, but I've been told there was light. I've been told what it was like, though my memory won't allow the images to surface. My mind stretches back to this foreign place with all of its tunnels and illusions, all of its hidden mysteries. Standing there together, in a slow-moving confusion, we could make out the warrens and hideouts of the desert's design, the places coyotes went at night, clouds of dust billowing up from cars and trucks quickly escaping back to water, people, homes. We surveyed the sky, immeasurable in its distance, hovering over this cache of desert mountains, what could have been painted impressions or dusty memories.

*

We wouldn't shower for days. We would carry the desert home with us, lingering before we cleaned ourselves, standing in doorways remembering what we had seen, peeling our clothes off, examining our hands, touching the dust on our knees and toes.

*

I want to know what this place represents, why the experience suggests to me now, a certain yearning. The tunnel was a force that drew us in, pressed into us a riddle we needed to solve: *Who am I?* We needed this tunnel as much as the man who dug it. Something outside of our ordinary lives. A retreat into nowhere. Some event that might form who we were as individuals, an exercise in mystery, one we could bring back home to say this was us. But perhaps I'm filling this story with meaning and it has none. Maybe the meaning lies in the place and that's it. And yet, I want to say I went to learn the weight of desire, of sadness, both in place and man, and to witness a justified beauty in the terrible quiet of that empty mountain.

*

Today, almost twenty years later, the others re-tell the story with confidence, but a certain vagueness persists, just as my memory tricks me. Many versions of the story exist, but this part is clear: we emerged from the tunnel onto a perch of rock, the whole span of desert reaching for hundreds of miles in front of us, full and rich, a shock of beauty we all remember. The miner must have seen such beauty with that last knock of rock. Did he cry out with relief? Did he fall to the dirt and sigh and watch as those open skies unfurled into endless tumbleweed and dream? Did he wonder what was real? What was not?

27

Of Youth

I want to go back to when I had soft hair parted in the middle with blue barrettes and ribbons. I want to go back to pink shirts, blue jeans with the cuffs rolled, tennis shoes, and the red cooler with the top off, my dad with a beer in his hand. I want to go back to the sand, to the weeds growing out of the rocks, my hand considering the stem, all the world a science project. In an old photo, my father stands behind me pointing to a line of trees. I am just six, maybe not even. My brother hunches in the sand, and the red willow branches fire up the sky. It looks like acres of corn behind us and a canvas of blue sky waiting to be filled in. It isn't that I'm just nostalgic, wanting to be a girl again. It's because I sometimes believe I never grew up. Where we lived, there was a roll of hill that led to the trees, a slow build of wood and lumber, a storming of mice, a bullfrog deep in its watery den, thunder arriving from the plains. The woods rolled around me, us, our family, the many neighborhood families in their homes that stood lonely. There was something rare in those woods, the graceful sweep of hickory and oak, goldenrod and milkweed—willowy, robust and dangerous, like a waltz.

28

(I always feel when one person is indebted to another for something very special, that indebtedness should remain a secret between just the two of them.—Rilke)

Letter to Lou Salomé (Rilke's lover) (1):

I recognized a few things on my walk today—a day I had originally met with hesitancy, but which came with a spilling of leaves like rapid rain—no, like feathers from a million geese moving on for the season, a day which came with rosehips bleeding away against the hour, the essence of the air brilliant with an oncoming spoil, everything too beautiful to be even real or tangible, but over there was a real tree, a real sky, a real mountain, all of this surrounding me without flaw. I passed an abandoned homestead along the way, a house with no one in it, the old man dead, his family in conflict over the place now falling apart. The silence broke when Josh came to me and wanted to hold my hand, wanted me to want him. I wanted him to go away. I wanted him to disappear. I wanted my secrets and my own kingdom of quiet. What did you mean when you wrote to Rilke: *There is something in it as of a newly conquered domain, one whose boundaries are still out beyond one's ken, its compass extending farther than one could walk: one senses more terrain?* You mean love as the domain, the sense of expansiveness love brings as some sort of distance? Sometimes it's easier not to talk, I think. I want to tell you that M_, my new lover, and I danced, and there were just the fingers, and the music, and the

fierce energy between us. Love or passion we didn't know. Like this,
*Your body knew of its coming, as it were, before you yourself did, yet
in the way that only bodies know of things*—it's as if the body cannot
resist what it knows. I've been thinking about how we don't do things,
for whatever reasons we come up with: rejection, loss, hurt, I think,
fear. I've been thinking about this not-doing and also the stories
composed in each walk and conversation and dance. *We are
erotically fired to subsume things of the body into the meanings of art.*
Is that what this all is? For art? Lou, there was a man who lived on my
road and every day he walked to the gas stop and café, a mile down
from the trailer park where he lived, to purchase beer, chips, smokes.
This man wore all black. No hat. He looked like death would if it
were a man, nearly seven feet in height, I wanted to believe. He was
thinner than a broom handle, thinner than an olive branch. He was so
thin it was almost as if he didn't exist. He smoked while he walked,
not looking in any one direction, but straight ahead, appeared as if he
was looking into nowhere, or nothing. He was sad, I could tell. And in
this sadness was death. I stood in line behind him at the station,
watched the way he placed groceries onto the counter, slowly, as if the
effort to lift his arms was more pain than his body could endure. He
barely made a whisper with his breath. He purchased soda, maybe a
tall can of beer, asked for a pack of cigarettes, I don't remember
which kind. Every day I saw him, until I no longer did. I expect he
died. I haven't seen him since, which makes me think that he was in
fact dying along the road, every day walking that much closer to his
death. . . . *we want to hold tightly to the things that are most dreadful*

about our circumstances, don't want to let go despite all the suffering. Maybe it needs to start with a story: I sat with Josh at the bar of a local diner, eating eggs and toast as if nothing had ever happened between us. As if I hadn't slept with another man. I placed my hand on his leg. The rain came down hard like some sheltering kind of storm. It was nice to sip tea in the window, not to worry about other relationships, men. Just the two of us together in a storm. But, he wouldn't let me in, accept the hand on his leg. He smiled sadly at the rain, told me, "It's over. We're dead."

29

Of Youth, Part Two

I was twelve when several of us talked about fleeing to the cave for a night. A cave with bats and rocks and shadowy things. A cave up in the blistering hills, where the coyotes hunted, where the scrub and needles scraped the wind. One of the boys knew how to get there. We could ride our bikes most of the way, walk the final distance. I didn't think I could really go (how, I wondered, when I was to be at home in bed?), but I said okay. I liked rain gathering in the afternoon and reading romance novels by the window, but I didn't know about caves. I guess if the others . . . We made plans at recess, when the tetherball spun through the air while we watched it, while the pavement burned creating a mirage of heat like shaking glass. I didn't know what we'd do once we arrived at the cave. I hoped for storytelling. Maybe kisses. Maybe new touch. We split the provisions—I'd bring cigarettes because my mother would never know. At school in the field atop the thinly mowed sod, we put our heads close, whispered about candles, matches, crackers, sweatshirts. We were scared but we cared for adventure. I want to say now that the cave was just a fantasy, a narrative dream threaded together for the adrenaline of imagining it. I remember the afternoon of last hours before we were to go. I remember looking across the school field and over the juniper and eucalyptus to a woman in the window of her split two-story house swaying with her baby, to music I thought, watching the school kids clustered about with all of their longing, on the threshold of what they didn't know, in search of what they couldn't understand.

30

On Identity: The Farmer's Wife, Etc.

—Kale, *Brassica oleracea*

"and she will not say how there

  must be more to living

  than this brief bright bridge"

    —from *The Farmer's Wife*, Anne Sexton

A lady, wrapped in black silk, called me the farmer's wife. Josh and I were hosting a party, a celebration for two hundred in the dirt with food we grew on the table: tomato confit, radicchio salad, basil tapenade. Perhaps I appeared to her as a model of the aproned woman, though only the chefs and servers wore aprons on this day. Perhaps she thought she should comment on me like you might a dog, a cow, a rare sighting of some egret or heron arriving unexpectedly to the party. I smiled as a kindness. This was my farm and I couldn't dismiss her. I was the hostess, after all, and what should a hostess do but make guests feel comfortable, welcome? I smiled to her and wandered toward the fence along the river to sip my rose wine, thinking of such classification: the farmer's wife.

From Hume, 1739: Of all relations the most universal is that of identity, being common to every being, whose existence has any duration.

We've all known the farmer's wife—from film, story. We think she wears aprons, sweeps dirt from the stoop, chases children around the yard. She keeps chickens and plants seeds in the garden, clips herbs for dinner. She makes biscuits and pies. She is more than gracious when we stop by to say hello. We know that she keeps everything in order. But there is another story beyond the stereotype. It isn't just the daily chores that make her. Perhaps she hides money in drawers or reads books when no one is looking. She might scribble in notebooks or dream beyond the front porch—of freedom, of wealth, of fame, who knows? Can we minimize the farmer's wife to just the chores she finishes on her daily to-do list? Could this woman identify me as such? What did this woman, a guest on my farm, know of me, of my dreams? I think of the great literary women whose lives were busy with children and stole moments to write: Clarice Lispector, Shirley Jackson, Toni Morrison. I wanted to turn to that woman and tell her of all my many selves: the girl who was expelled from Catholic school, the girl who always liked to break the rules, the woman who ran away from home into the dark streets of her hometown, the woman who smoked and talked Marxism and social justice in college, who wrote poetry at dawn, who desperately wanted to be subversive. The rebel. The writer. The DJ. I thought it was important for her to know these things. I clung to the import of defining my identity, the characteristics of a self being the chief categorization: my mannerisms, my story, the elements of my core. Who am I? What is this self? Where do I fit in?

I turned toward the congregation of guests gathered in the waning afternoon. The sun had tipped behind the trees framing the lines of kale and cabbage all in evening glow, their tufts and flowers outlining the sky. Plates clanked on a long table that stretched between nine sections of irrigation pipe, three hundred feet in all. Glasses, knives, forks, creamers, and antique lamps had been set among the day which clung to the night, the river curled and wide beside us. All of the evening's shadows moved west in a creeping gray light. The trees hosted a trick of birds. A gunshot took off in the distance. We conversed mainly in acquaintances. The air buzzed with voices and talk. Josh toasted the crowd, "This is the longest table I've ever sat at." There was so much they didn't know. I looked away from the table of people who glanced at me, to my son who climbed over the antique thing of a tractor and watched as he chewed a rolled-up salad of tatsoi leaves, leek shoots, and purslane flowers. She called me the farmer's wife. My identity defined by my husband. I thought, I am not just one story. I'm not just a farmer's wife, though at times I guess that is what distinguishes me from the rest. Often, whether I know or don't know, my identity is defined by my husband—that's why the woman called me so. For her, I appeared to be just the farmer's wife, nothing else in that moment, only the wife out for a night, stealing away with her glass of wine, savoring the evening and the break from chores, from caregiving, from all that makes her the farmer's wife.

From Alden, 1866: The idea of identity is involved in every act of remembrance.

When I was a girl, I read *Little House on the Prairie* and, probably like so many other girls, I romanticized farm life, dreaming up scenes of my rural wedding to some unknown farmer. In my reverie, I rode horses on the range, made butter, wore aprons and prairie dresses—the whole lot. I turned out golden on an expanse of sky so large I couldn't see the end. In reality, I lived in the suburbs of southern California. I swam in chlorine pools, shuffled around the Santa Ana mall, and flipped hair on the couch while watching television shows and movies, all of me becoming increasingly bored as the years moved on. I was so far removed from the country that how I got here, how I stand on a patch of land that rolls with the wind, still confounds me. It is often difficult to distinguish the origin of my burgeoning fantasies of countryside bliss.

As I grew older, I sat in my pink room with my lace coverlet pulled over my legs and mused over my country husband. I imagined him, large and bulky with a long, dark beard that scratched my face at night while we made love and our wild children slept under a cradled moon—the house warm from the wood fire, the candles dripping wax on the table, the teapot burning on the stovetop, the cups empty and forgotten in the space of our love. In my dreams, my country husband wore trousers with suspenders and lovingly chopped wood, hauled nails and hammers, brought in the harvest, loved me completely, with abandon and without restraint. This isn't far from the truth now.

In Marcel Duchamp's painting "Nude Descending a Stairs," a figure is represented by a mixture and blend of ochre and brown. It's complex, this painting, many shapes and sharp edges defining the movement of a person. You can't tell that it is any one thing, just a series of shapes, octagons, triangles, but the painting is a reflection of the multiple self, an interpretation of our multiple identities. Like the nude in the painting, I was born of contrasts, under the sign of Gemini represented by the twins. Duality. The struggle and pull between two selves. I'd always wrestled with the idea of self, searching for the peace of "This is who I am," though I knew I'd never find it.

When I traveled to Puerto Rico for the first time, a trip destined to undo my marriage, I tried on a new self, shed the old label of the farmers' wife, which felt as cracked as the cobble of the Puerto Rican streets—iron slag, stuck through with purslane. It was there, on that island, the new self was born. This new woman who would love and desire without regret. I had travelled with a group of students and faculty, exploring the literature of the island, learning of Julia de Burgos, whose poem to herself inspired my own particular exploration. She wrote, "You belong to your husband, your master; not me;/I belong to nobody, or all, because to all, to all/I give myself in my clean feeling and in my thought...Not in me, in me only my heart governs,/only my thought; who governs in me is me." I sat on a terrace above the streets of San Juan and decided I'd leave Josh. That to be a free woman, I must unlock from marriage, and as Burgos did, govern only myself. This new self, though, was fine and uncertain, a little bit fragile. Her strength hid in the language of the island, in the spines of the books, in the romance of living a life of freedom, though Burgos herself died alone in the streets.

One afternoon, I met a beautiful bohemian, a woman adorned in layered cloth and jewels, hair dreaded into a ponytail atop her head. From her, I bought a bracelet of brown thread—turquoise, indigo, hazel—woven into stitches around a jade stone, the mineral of nephrite, streaked with ivory, the gem sized to that of a tree frog or the eye of a hippo, something wild and almost out of place on my small arm, which pushed against my fair skin making marks and impressions where it wrapped me in its charm. I paid too much for it—eighty-five dollars after a short negotiation—but my dear friend, a woman of fair skin and fiery red hair, pushed me to purchase it. She said, "You need a talisman. Something to take home with you. To remember who you are now." I trusted she was right, so I counted the cash and with the transaction finished, I took the bracelet with me into the cobblestone streets where I admired its strength, the colors of earth combining to enrich a firm guide in some direction toward love or beauty. I wear it still.

From Segal, 1918: Love is the feeling of or sense of identity with the pain of another.

A fairy tale tells one story—"The Marriage of Sir Gawain and the Lady Ragnell" —of what women want beyond all else. The story goes that, in order to save his life, King Arthur must answer the question, "What do women desire above all else?" Most men think women desire to be beautiful, or desire attention from men, or further, hold a finite desire to be wed and wifed. All true, but what King Arthur learns from Lady Ragnell is that women, above all else, desire to exercise their own free will, to hold their own power of sovereignty. I needed desire like I needed water, my shoes, my own breath. And more than desire, as Lady Ragnell suggested, I needed freedom. I'm not special. This is not new, but it was new to me, so I broke everything I knew about myself and my marriage to discover how I could be a free woman.

I thought I could live between two men. I possessed the space to explore. I felt entitled to it, I suppose, but there's something about this pairing that isn't quite right—

First moon: I was with Josh, lying in an orchard of grass and apple with a wide moon above, like a ball of basalt, our desire taking shape in the dented grass, in the glasses of red wine laid on their side, bugs crawling into the sediment around us. Desire taking shape in his mouth and mine, in the conversation, in his eyes that reflected a universe of nuance and adoration. Of me. Why? And then the owls, a duplet in silence, not even a whisper of wing between the two, just a silhouette, just a quick shadow and then gone into the trees. I want to say the owls represented that broken desire between us, the way lips push into each other, the way we took that wine, the way we drank it like a smooth syrup, took our time getting to know each arm, elbow. After so many years. Or maybe those owls spoke the half-truths because we can't reveal it all: what we fear, what we don't know, what we think we know, the prosaic. I wondered about what could harm us. I wanted the owls to be something mystical for us, to show us which way to follow: the wind, our dreams, that unclaimed desire.

Second moon: I was with the lover. I hadn't heard *Dreams* in years, but he put it on the stereo, the lights dimmed low. We were naked by then, sharing a glass of whiskey, the brand of which I can't remember now. His sheets were black. His blanket was black. His hair was black. The moon was full. Thirty days after the husband's moon. "Do you know the graffiti artist Banksy?" We had been looking at photos of his trip to Europe before stripping our clothes. He was nervous pulling out posters and books and souvenirs to show me. Fumbling for a hat. Making jokes about geography. Prussia. He said, "What do you call . . . ?" I mentioned my boat ride with Finnish punks on a cruiser with Josh after college. That early time, that December, we'd gone to bed with each other twice, and we were new, just getting to know the other's body. He was everything Josh wasn't: living in a hollow of a cabin with no job, no ambition. Most of the time we were very drunk. Most of the time we fell on the floor from too much wrestling. The moon was full, did I say that. This night, he had stopped our lovemaking, just like that, grabbed his glass of whiskey, and started a conversation about Joni Mitchell. "I seem to love women who sing best. I don't know. Because I love the way their voices make me calm." Stevie Nicks in the air: "Now here you go again, you say you want your freedom/Well who am I to keep you down/It's only right that you should/Play the way you feel it." I told Josh I'd be home at one. Thirty-seven years old and I had a curfew. He was home with the children, sitting by the fire, drinking, wondering what he'd done with his wife, how she'd gone away. That other self. Her new self with the lover, certain in the choice she was making, though her husband did not know.

From W. Irving, 1819, Rip Van Winkle: He doubted his own identity, and whether he was himself or another man.

I wonder, do trees doubt their own ability to root? I doubted my size, the value of my beauty and how to have a new lover. There was a memory of my many sizes over time, from a waist of twenty to six. I used to be large and now I wasn't. In math, identity = a relationship between A and B, of the same functions. I don't know math, but the variability of two people is what matters, and the relationship that fuses their identities, one in reflection of the other, and the need to feel beautiful, to leave doubt to math or science, some hypothesis that might prove sureness and certainty.

Later with the lover—through white curtains, thin and see-through, no privacy, no cover—the morning comes through warm, and in that, the doubt of my body, my beauty, my self, exposed breasts and fleshy legs. Josh always loved my body. Did this lover love it the same? If at all? And where are the children?

A memory from early in my marriage comes to me while I lay there: a day when lightning struck the ground and from it, fire. The pine needles flared. The trees burned. The animals ran. The air became smoke, the world transformed, becoming new, like a planet that has never been. Lying there with the lover, discussing basketball and radio, I remembered this day of fire, the sun and clouds shifting directions, the sky appearing as if it were building to go extinct with power lines illuminated and the sky purple and black and devastating. The sun came down through a fiery pink thread of clouds. My children in the back of a car. I remember thinking, I'm not meant for this, I'm not meant for any of this, this burden of domesticity, of mother and wife, of what is a family, but then Everett called to me, "The lightning is striking and we better move because if we don't, then we won't ever make it home." He was anxious, his forehead creased, the tone in his voice urgent. At six, he felt the world like this, in all of its terrible elemental darkness. I thought, No, this is okay. This is just right. I love him and he loves me and this is all I need, but I recognize this sounds like a persuasion of some kind, as if I needed to be convinced. Should I tell the lover this memory?

I tell the lover the memory and we discuss the many ways to remember fire—at camp with marshmallows and guitar songs and rolled cigarettes; at the winter solstice when children run with lanterns through the dead grass and we light piles of wood and debris on the hill and watch our faces glow in the light then sip spiked cider and eat soup; at a house in Missoula in a ring in the backyard where the alley cats came to sit on the fence while we talked about weathered tables to sell, or other things like futures; or at a friend's land, when I was just young, when nothing was of worry, where we gathered to burn trash and paper and wood and drink booze and my dying friend, he told me to sing, to keep singing the song he loved to hear, and so I did. I sang and then we hiked the hill behind the fire and he couldn't make it up because he was tired and dying, so I left him to trail behind me because I didn't know what to say to a friend who was dying, so I kept walking higher up the mountain. He stood there in the trees and shadows, a ghostly shape, heaving under the wicked and cruel moon.

From Charlotte Bronte: I am no bird; and no net ensnares me.

I drove with my mother one afternoon returning from a visit with Everett's preschool teacher. We discussed the state of our farm and she turned to me and said, "I just always imagined you would marry a professor and make something more of your life, but you married a farmer and I never once thought that your life would be so hard. I never thought you would be so poor." Her face creased into worry lines, the wrinkles of her eyes folded over each other. She leaned forward in her seat to catch my eye, slumping like she was reaching for an item dropped on the floor mats. My children slept in the back seat, Ava's head also slumped and awkward. I replied, "We're not poor!" She said, "You don't even have toilet paper in the house." I kept driving, adjusted the rear-view mirror and turned up the radio. She stared at me for a long time, but I didn't look, just kept at the road and watched the sprinklers shoot water on the pear trees.

The farmer's wife is always more than we think she is.

31

As Snow Designs, or the Narrator on Loss

Begin here,

If there was something to mention in the first sentence, to set a scene, it would be the back streets: how they shaped the rows of houses, their geometry performed in straight lines as if you could cut them with scissors and collage them into another map. You could make a different city. These alleys accommodated many things, like lilac bushes and broken fences, cats on rooftops, puddles with pebbles overcome with the aftermath of a spilling storm, children with voices that reached out and spun to the chimneys. Each of the homes with their collective alleyways contained a view, but my take was to the hill by the college, the one with the "M" sketched in white across the side slant, reached only by climbing a steep trail to the top, from which one could take in the spread of valley dotted with marks and blemish of grass, both dead and growing, both still and becoming. This valley stored ranches, box stores, parking lots, bars, bridges, and, far off, a woman holding a baby next to her chest, so close, like a packaged gift: the breath of such a life small and vital on the air around which the world passes by without thought, without recognition of, or response to, the beauty of such an image. But that would be only one way to start.

No, this is better,

In an afternoon silver with trees and no birds, a storm came too fast spreading snow across the sidewalks. It came so fast there was no time to prepare. I walked quickly from campus through the snowy Missoula streets, huddled against the cold without a proper jacket. I felt the possibility of loss as an exertion of pressure on my chest as I walked, the force overwhelming like I was to be swallowed into the buried sky. This loss as an interruption to the ordinary. Josh had gone to the mountains with two friends hours before. I wondered about them in the woods with the snow. I wondered about the blurry confusion of a quick storm. You could say I was worried. As a couple, we were so new, our love like fresh soap taken from the plastic and sweet like lavender. What little we knew of snow in those mountains, of anything really, like love and forgiveness, forgetting, or worse, this thing I wonder about: loss. I learned that in physics, loss is "a reduction of power within or among circuits, measured as a ratio of power input to power output." I want this definition to be generic. Circuits, as in the way we are tied together. When you love, you lose. So then.

When he didn't return from the hike he set out on, when the snow kept coming and the day darkened with violet overtones and wrenched gray, when I opened that beer and took the taste of hops down my throat, so too the circuitry of my power dulled, everything in me equalizing, reduced to nothing—all my bones, my skin, my body without influence. I was paralyzed with worry. The only thing I could do was watch the storm bury my car, and the children across the street who were busy building a snowman. They laughed as they placed stick arms onto the figure's torso. Maybe they argued about whose scarf they could abandon to their art. I could have gone to them, or to the road, stood there and waited for the snow to bury me like it would bury him and the snowman and the children rolling balls. I could have stayed there for a long time and let the snow stick to my hands, or hair, or boots, and leave my love to the snow just like that. Let it unfold as it would.

Or,

To think about loss first is another way to tell the story, before the snow, and in particular, when anything—cars, wind, fall, razor, saw, etc.—arrives hard and fast without thinking about you or anyone else you love. Events that break a life just like that. I could use the phrase *A blink of the eye* or *In a flash* to tell you the haste of loss, but these say nothing of the tension or speed of devastation because they are so ordinary, so, I don't know, dull. We say them every day. No, what I'm talking about is that moment when you remember that, yes, we all lose somebody at some point. There are reasons that afternoon of snow has thickened into my mind, why I recall it now almost as acutely as the day it occurred. My heart beats still to think about the terror, about the tug of being alone, about the dark house without my love in it, about the empty leftovers of the day's warning, the snow itself a caution: be careful who you let in and always be prepared to let go.

I once saw a man on the street, a performer painted all silver—his face, his arms, his hair—and when I passed by him, he didn't move, but stayed lodged in place, unmoving and impassive, his eyes fixed onto the steeple of the building across the way. I stopped to watch. We stood there for a long time together. Minutes passed. The sidewalks filled and emptied. The light shifted to the window behind me. I remember looking to the people around me and wondering if they wondered as much as I did about the man behind the silver, wondered what he had lost, if he had lost, and what had they lost and isn't it just this community of loss that traces us all together? This collective losing. After a while, I thought it must be time to go; I had stood there too long already and who was this girl who wouldn't budge from the sidewalk and move on to the small insignificances of her own life? Her bag was heavy; she must have had somewhere to go even as she lifted the bag and realized the silver man had slowly shifted his position over the minutes she had been standing there, without her notice or attention, his silver body now entirely placed to the east, to her, his eyes designing what she could never know.

On second thought,

There's something to be said about departures. This is a different kind of beginning. I think about how our loyalty holds us, our devotion to each other remains strong in ways I sometimes don't understand. I was devoted to Josh, so I went to find him on that afternoon, despite the uselessness of such a search. How was I to find him in the snow? I didn't know where he had gone, carried only a vague notion, but I went anyway, in the dark, driving over wet pavement, gripping the steering wheel with just wool gloves, maybe I wore a hat, and I took the truck because it could navigate the way better. I waited for a long time before leaving, the snow almost too much to drive in by then, beer on my breath still, a possibility of highway interruptions like police or car crashes or a woman crossing the street with her baby in the snow, I'm not sure. But then he came back to me, or I him, coming down the road in our friend's big truck as I rambled toward the mountains. He returned, as many do who wander in the wilderness, as some don't, the possible loss just a distance now, not even in the consciousness of that day, so quickly gone to the past. He appeared in the glow of my headlights, his figure appearing in the front seat of my friend's car. The driver rolled down the window and I looked to my lover and thought his legs must be shaky from walking for hours, tense too, the core of his body cold and uncertain and scared and the snow still spreading against the windows as I thought of something to say. There was nothing to say. I didn't say anything, or maybe it was, "Where have you been?" or "What happened?" and the chaos and relief of return was burdened by his stiff back and frozen fingers. I didn't speak for a long time at the pub as he devoured two hamburgers, a beer, fries, everything he had before him on that table, his attempt at glut, at satisfaction so obvious: a need to extinguish a disappearance or loss, that could have been, but wasn't.

Whatever. This isn't working,

I think my fear of loss on that snowy afternoon could be as lonely as the vulnerability of standing with the silver performer and meeting his eyes in expectation of what he might find. What could he find? The loss I have felt. The worry. It could be as lonely as the pain of a death. The fear as big as the mountains or the dark. The fear as big as the silver man still standing there forever staring at me. The fear of everything that could be gone or revealed or unearthed or taken.

Here's what I can imagine of Josh's experience: maybe he thought of ways he could survive. He didn't tell me so, but maybe he could have found a tree to crawl under. To dig out the snow, curl up next to the bark, remember what waited for him at home: me. The youth he still had. The land he hoped to work in the future. He might have thought about how to start a fire with wet tinder all around. He might have thought about building a shelter of sticks. Maybe he wanted to do something with his hands. To keep busy. Maybe he only wanted to be found. He would be restless or cold and sad, but then maybe the snow would keep him company, and the dog too, the black dog with her warmth, would radiate to him and maybe he would have laid his head on her back and that would be enough. He might make note of things he would say to me if he could.

This must be the end then,

I suppose we've all walked into the snow, let it come quickly and cover us, allowing us to think of anything we've ever lost: a slipper shoved under the couch; a wallet in the crease of a car; Ava, unwound in her jackets and backpack in the stacks of the library, sitting on the carpet with just the books surrounding her, her loss felt in the spine of a book, in the story and the words that come up off the page. Loss upon leaving a place. Loss like a porcelain sink holding water until it doesn't and you let the drain go, and let all of whatever's left flow away down into the pipes to the sewers. But these are the small losses. Losing someone into the snow, or a daughter in the crowded mall where only a stranger can undo the day, or the death of a lover: these are the losses that count. It is the expectation of loss, the fear, that feeling in the pit of your abdomen, like heavy sand, like ice that rules the heart. This sink of sadness feels like everything and nothing at once, so much that it allows me to recall the people I have lost: a good friend to the cliffs, another friend to cancer in his hips, a grandmother to old age. I wrote a wisteria poem for her when she died. I swam naked in an ocean for my friends. I remember them. Is that enough? This reminder of loss allows me to love a man who could someday fall away into the snow. I love him for many things: the weight of his heart; the evidence of his life on the folds of his skin near his eyes; hands hewn like brick, like stone, like all the mixings of a strong building; the fiery look that passes onto his face when he's frustrated or troubled; or just the way he walks down the driveway holding our daughter's small hand.

32

Murmur, or the Narrator on Love

Until we find each other, we are alone[2], as the heart's incantations
prove in the low hum of its daily clock, always beating until it doesn't.
This heart tempo quickens upon the arrival of love, upon seeing the
one you love, upon love. There are many ways to place love in the
night: a whisper or hushed "let me touch your back," something like
the timbre of a violin, the soloist plucking the strings looking for some
kind of friendship or affection; between the skin, or a purl, a purr, an
attachment of lips underneath wool in the dark—that kind of sound.
An almost *notsound*: undertone of sex, the scene of bodies twisted on
the terrain of the marital bed, continual impulse and the erotic
suggestion. We are victims here, always succumbing to the motion of
desire and the flutter of tail feathers from the finch before an island
morning breaks. I have a son. I have a daughter. I have a man I love,
their father, who will come to an end eventually and apart from me,
but for now, we collect ourselves into a framed house with a sort of
music that's as repeatable as the day's headlines. We create this
music. A family of refrains. On our farm, a road cuts through the
middle, splitting the landscape into two. We can call it a pair of farms
then, bisecting the world: the house, the barn, the creek to one side;

---

[2] -with *Adrienne Rich*

the other a slope of rye and timothy, an ancient apple tree unpruned, wild rose, cedar, our dog's bones (she's been gone for years), yarrow and lily, all suffering their own decay as protracted sighs to the earth. On this road, the ground is made of sediment, from where I don't know, and I cover it with petals, blush and rose, pulled from my handbag where the blooms have come apart from the stems. Ava and I sprinkle the gravel with these segments. They color our path, creating a quiet chapter to follow home. They form a chain to which I can offer you this: along the Pacific Northwest shore, I came upon a creature, a salp, a pelagic artifact, related to the open sea, existing in the upper layers and channels of ocean. They are but objects of jelly, which clone into sequences, wheels, helixes. They suspend into gorgeous chains, arrive to the shore eventually where they cap the beach with their backbones. It's the tideline that whispers of this fact: we can perceive the universe in the smallest of things, as if in a slow chant or a drawn-out progression of tender moments or the shutting of a door when it's too late and you haven't said goodbye yet. *Don't go*, whispered to the one you love. It's said the salps, abandoned to the sand, tell of imbalance and the strike of man on our own ecology. I want to become a kind of private witness that forgets this death or mourns this loss with a rhythm felt as deep as the bodies' middle. Right there where the belly moans. I want love. Near the shore and the salps and the sand, at Emmanuel's Episcopalian Church, I discovered a labyrinth: I did not skip or dance or crawl. I clicked my boots along the track. I tried to meet with my soul as suggested by the handbill. I learned, then, a labyrinth does not have walls, no tricks or dead ends, the entrance is also the exit, creating a design of reflection, stance, originally conceived and designed by Daedalus to capture the minotaur. What is a minotaur but a duality of identity, a metaphor for the violence of man, or a creature misunderstood, containing complexities in its physical form? And the labyrinth, a way to contain the wild? Here, the grass frames the stone, plain and short from summer's inattention. I drop four quarters in the slot before leaving, for luck or love or both, peek into the church's entry, and think of Mary Oliver's dying gull, whose adventure and curiosity cannot resist the collapse of its own body, when its wounded feet shrivel and it dies, looking out the window, unable to fly.

33

(It is not enough for two people to find each other, it is also very important that they find each other at the right moment and hold deep, quiet festivals in which their desires merge so they can fight as one against storms.—Rilke)

Letter to Lou Salomé (2):

Josh and I fight again when the morning has rain and there is nothing left to say. I look for rentals online. I ask about prices. I calculate the bills, the risk. What I'll let go. He smashes the new beer glasses I bought for him in the sink. I pick the glass from the porcelain being sure not to cut my fingers. There isn't any blood, no trace of red when I place the pieces in the trash. He leaves, taking the tent, the sleeping bag, the car. I know he'll have a good time wherever he goes without me.

*

Later, I return home from a trip, too late from a plane that was delayed, from a sky that was cloudy, bumpy, terrifying and beautiful at once. I climb into bed. I give him my body, but he doesn't turn, doesn't touch me and it's cold. I cannot flourish here.

*

The cold has landed, the birds have gone away, and I still haven't cut the lavender down, even though summer has passed. I went to visit my brother who lives in a canyon with palm trees and oaks and a dog and red wine that never finishes and we talked over jazz and blues, Miles Davis mainly. He asked about my book. He asked what I write. He asked what it's like to be married. I told him all that I could, an inventory of my courage.

*

The house is quiet. The wood stove pops with its fire. I put whiskey in my tea. He doesn't. We drink in separate rooms. I go outside. I smoke a cigarette. He joins me, turning on the twinkle lights in our outdoor kitchen. I get up to leave. Say, I already had two cigarettes. There is a Christmas tree, but it means nothing. To the children, maybe, it signals joy, but our son can't sleep at night. He wakes at two, three, four in the morning. I hear him wandering through the house. I wake, think I should go to him, but he knows how to pour milk, turn on a story, peel the mandarins because now is the season for such fruit. He'll leave the peels on the couch, tucked into the cushions where I will find them later like little discards of color against the gray.

*

At two in the morning, our voices are heard like echoes through the house. Everett whimpers in his bed. I know he's tuned to the things we say to each other, so I lay with him and stroke his cheeks, his hair, his forehead. I wipe his tears with my fingers. I put them on my face so I can feel them too. I say, "It's okay. Go to sleep." His face all wet, all beautiful. So soft. He says, "Is it over?" I reply, "No, no. Everything's okay." But I know better. I know more than him, and what can I say? He's afraid. He wanders the house like a ghost, all hours of the morning, his tiny feet big drums in my ears.

*

I drive to the store to buy wrapping paper, but I can't do it. I turn away from the store, walk to my car, open the door, sit in the driver's seat, turn the ignition. I wait and look at the sky, which has never given me anything but blue and gray, some spectrum of color too, though it is difficult to access this scale of hues in the car. I look at the liquor on the seat beside me. There are two kinds of whiskey, Drambuie, Irish cream. I will pour the spirits into my glass on Christmas Eve and think about when we first kissed under a moon on a pallet of down and wood and Santa Cruz mist with cocaine in our blood. He said to me back then, "I can't believe how beautiful you are." Later, after leaving the store with the liquor, I read your book in the cold and imagine your love with Rilke: *As we walked on* [Rilke and Lou], *barefoot, quietly, we found deep in the overgrown forest an open place whose tangles of light-brown shriveled fern lay all about, like embers that had wafted down between the tree trunks, sun-embers.*

*

I'll think about this time with regret, or relief maybe, or how the months just seemed to turn into years without ever having written them down in my datebooks, my calendars, ever having taken notice. I'm a foolish woman, I think, for giving up such love, because who will want me when I'm old? My body is marked with stretches and dimples of fat. No one will want me. I'm a foolish woman, I think, for these questions and anxieties. Why do they matter? History haunts me: who to be as a wife, as a woman, as writer, as lover.

He points his finger at me as I lay against the pillows on our bed. My back hurts. My neck too. He says, "You're the one who's fucking another man." I think about pointing, about all the ways it strikes, condemns, and implicates. A baby points early on, for desire, to express a state of need. Primates point. Dogs. Elephants. I tremble to the rage. I cower to the pillows. He has shamed me, all blame and hex.

*

I arrive home at seven in the morning from a late party, after going to the lover's cabin. I hide the lover's shoes, his phone, his two shirts under the down jacket I took with me, push them into my drawers where Josh won't know. We had stripped our clothes in the car the night before, not having the patience to wait for another shelter. Everett asks, "Are you just getting home?" I laugh and hug him. "Yes, I guess so. I am." I tumble into bed, but Josh comes to me, doesn't understand where I've been. I don't care, Lou, but I keep holding on to the comfort and safety of a life like it's something I have wished forever, but it's a dream, like those in the fountains I toss coins into for love. It's like that. Just a dream, nothing more.

*

I do the things I have to: feed the children, take them to school, pack lunches, pick them up, brush their hair, bathe them, make them happy in whatever small way I can. Still, nothing is said. It would be better for them without us together. They know we can't live this way. He calls a therapist, because I won't. She refers him to someone else and then another and then another and then it just never happens because I get lazy or no one is willing to talk or we can't get help or because I'm too lazy. It's a stalemate, and what's the use anyway? He loves me too much. I don't love him enough.

*

He makes plans to go out. Where?—I don't know. I grow jealous. I'm always the one that goes out, Lou. I try to watch something on the television, but I can't pay attention. I try to read. I wonder, where could he have gone? The other day, he vacuumed the children's room while it rained and I read a book and the children whined for crackers and snacks and water and I ignored them and wanted to go away like I always do. I told him I'm sad, affected by the rain, the season, the clouds. He said, "Do you want to talk about it?" So kind. I shook my head and walked away. I didn't want him, but when he's away I do. I'm never sure how to live with that contradiction.

*

I read from a book that a boy is ready to be on his own when he's seven. Everett is seven. That means I can go. That means he'll be okay. He doesn't need me except when he goes to bed when he asks to hug twice. He asks for his light, his notebook, his pen, the covers. He calls to me when I'm reading in the other room. "Water?" "Hug?" "Bathroom?" Whatever he can muster. Anything, because the elephant and the moose and the giraffe, none of them can help him anymore and I wonder, isn't a boy ready to be alone at seven?

*

And then I remember why this isn't working. I look at the house with the children sleeping in it. I look at the moon outside. I remember this isn't what I want. I tell myself over and over and over again so I have the courage to leave. I think no one will love me again like he's loved me. But he's finished with my longings. When I run outside into the rain without shoes to chase him, I call to him. Stay, I say. He keeps going.

*

Again, the fire in the stove. The Christmas tree lit with red and pink and blue. The gifts unwrapped. I paint my toenails purple. I had gone to the store and bought a new dress. I tried to look pretty, and he says so, and I wished it meant something, but it doesn't anymore. I leave on a plane and it feels better to leave than it feels to stay.

34

Things About That Night

—Ponderosa Pine, *Pinus ponderosa*

"I had no other future other than the telephone call fixing our next
appointment."
—Annie Ernaux, from *Simple Passion*

I

One night when she is alone and the sky cartwheels with those lonely
stars she can never fathom, she reads in a book that only through hard
work does beauty take its final radiant form. So music. So art. So
writing. So all the things we do to produce beauty, she thinks, even the
beauty of holding a man's hand after too much whiskey and too little
conversation. The feel of sweat lined in the palms. His skin satin and
tender from little labor. Unlike Josh's hard hands, the cuts and
scrapes, the wounds infected. There are the lover's eyes too, and the
way the air feels around her, so new, like she's never felt the cold
coming on so cold. This new lover. This new man. This new
everything. She thinks of the book of love poems she used to carry in
her college backpack, pink cover with a lady and wisp of shadow in
black and white, Pablo Neruda sonneting, "The moon lives in the
lining of your skin." She thinks this of him, though she doesn't know.
She knows nothing really except this addiction to wanting, so when

she arrives to the radio station, she queues the first songs to seduce anyone who listens. That's how she chooses what to play: a slow beat, maybe a heavy bass, then an echo of strings like violin or cello, a few symphonic lyrics. On the night he comes to her, she clocks her show at four hours, knowing they will need time to discover each other in the dark, embracing on the turf grass, their cigarettes still burning in the tin at their feet. She's already planning. Knows Josh will listen, but disregards this anyway. They'll speak into the airspace of radio, talk candy like Butterfingers and licorice, share the whiskey glass between them, the dim glint of the one bulb lighting their teeth and skin. The last songs will play out suggestive of two a.m. trysts and dimmed bedroom lamps, the songs extending their melody over prolonged minutes, enough to wake the squirrels and stimulate the owls because by then, they'll be touching. She wants to believe she is creating an affair through music, but it's not like they talk about it and it's not like he knows, but even so, there lies a suspicion, a hunch or notion, that what they're doing is wrong.

II

Later, she travels alone to a beach where she can write. She thinks she could sit in front of the sea for a long time, sketch the rocks onto paper, empty a bottle of wine, smoke, think about the way he looks at her. He knows more than he tells. What is this ability to intuit another? It's as if he had a perception of her inner life, that somehow, he knew more about her than she ever told—an immediate cognition or insight, which always made her uneasy. But she wanted him to know her. She could carry herself along with his eyes, a color she still can't discern, no matter how often she tried. He watched her. And this desire. The scope of it, as far off as the constellation of Taurus, of the Pleiades. She wanted to run with them, those stars and the magnitude, the ascension of all that gravity and float. Of desire, Alain de Botton wrote, "Desire can only thrive on the impossibility of mutuality." So all of this is just a false yearning? Absurd? Impractical? The light has gone except for on the bay where there is a single buoy bobbing the waves. If he was with her, they wouldn't have to talk or say anything, just let the silence hold them, or allow the wreck of water on the rocks to say it all. Or she might ask, "What would it be like to be cold in that ocean? What would it be like to sink below, let the seaweed tangle and drag us along the heave of sea?" Down and down and down to the fangtooth fish and tube worms. As far as they could go. To the sharks and squid. She sees the boats in the peninsula pitch and toss in the harbor, their masts pointed high and thin like thorns to that blue wide that holds us all in place. She shivers in her coat with the wind pushing its brawn around the bushes, her body. She sees the tide bring with it every shell and star. The deep night isn't far, she thinks. If he were here, she'd say, "Let's go inside. I promise to keep the lights low. Let you look at me in the shadows." She imagines the sun tipping to the other side of the earth, the furthest distance she can conjure in her mind, and all these false imaginings. She takes her phone out from her pocket, dials her husband's number.

III

It's that part of the day where she wants to meet the beauty head on, or just reach out the window and mold the hills into new shapes, an alternative landscape that might jumble the world just enough to shake her out of her daze. Wake up now. You are in a delusion of your own making. She's driving with Josh and they don't talk, but she imagines what she might tell him about the lover. How he prefers her on top. How he throws her around the bed. Out the passenger window, the mountains seam together as bodies lying in green layers, complex, the curves just as intense as her longings. She doesn't want to be all skin and round folds and wrinkles without something like this beauty and that desire fully realized. She's understanding this now. "What if sexuality precisely calls into question that opposition between nature and culture?" So, it's a matter of resistance to norm. Nature: the physical world. Culture: intellectual achievement. She finds herself in-between, in the vague terrain of dissent, a place she's always felt comfortable and at home. Yes to the flesh. No to the standard. Or better, in deference to the experience, to the beauty of two bodies in intimation and embrace, to the disarray of attraction. She turns to Josh, "Do we need milk at the store?"

IV

At the radio: his hands on her ass—bold for this man who came to her slowly, like a snake, a suspicious wolf. He moaned like a cat might purr. Twice. The sound of it vibrated between them like a composition of some complicated hum, a soundtrack to his erection, a quick hardening after only a few kisses. He shoved his tongue in her mouth, without grace, she thought, abrupt, as if he might slam the brakes at a red light. She was a woman, didn't he know? He put his hands in her hair, pushed her closer that way, a form of dominance she let him keep. She touched his chest then to feel his fat and muscle, his back, kissed his neck, the odor of him not what she imagined, something of smoke and sweat and bitter whiskey. He felt so much not her husband—no, he was his own history gathered into the skin of his hips, the grease of his stringy hair—everything unfamiliar. He wore a large belt, which he began to unbuckle. She didn't recognize any of this. The music beat from the speakers too, a slow jam and then it was over, just as quickly as it began: a natural hesitation occurred, something to make them pause. He pulled away, perhaps overcome, knowing they couldn't go farther. Later, when she returns home, Josh screams at her in a way that is so deafening, a treble of fear and panic, as if he will pounce on her, take everything away from her, as if he may ignite on fire. She cowers, she pleads, she whispers, "Please. Please stop. He's not a good kisser." He stops. It's quiet. They stare at each other. She looks away. He cries into his hands until he can't anymore, then leaves the house in a quiet that is acute and irretrievable.

V

Since they began, it's been a play of what she could never say. A cliché almost, the comedy of a commonplace affair. She wants to believe it's something more, significant, but she sees that it is not, and it disturbs her. She wants what they've done to be unique or stand-out in some way. She wants to feel proud, wants others to know she's carried herself as a woman who is strong and confident in her sexuality. But that's a lie. She's insignificant. With him, she's never felt despondent as a lover might, but more, infatuated with the unknown: of what he was doing, what he was saying, what he thought, what he was reading, who he was seeing, what he sensed about her. She's been thinking about what they did. She's been thinking about everything they said. She goes through it in her mind over and over again. He came to her like a dog, like a child to an embrace. She seduced him as she knew she could: gifts and treasures, notes, emails, suggestions on the air, texts with lines of poetry, short skirts, drink, music with bass, dance. She chose him because it was easy. She wonders, does desire earn an individual definition? Is that what this is? Desire, she reads, "is what remains unknown in the utterance." There were so many silences between them, but who left it quieter, she doesn't know. She often imagined him with his other lover, compared herself to this other woman who lived far away and what did they do and how did they do it and did they discuss her and was she better at sucking than she was and didn't he like her skin and eyes more because they were blue and indefinite?

VI

He lived alone in the woods with two black cats—cats to whom she feigned affection—a cabin tucked away from everything they both feared in the world: capitalism, war, crime, injustice. He kept his beer in a cooler out back, a low fence surrounding a lawn of weeds and grass. A generator fueled his lights, his stove, the radio. Bookshelves lined the walls with anarchist pamphlets and Ernest Hemingway and Italian philosophers. A bucket to shit in. She had dreamed of this cabin for months, wanted it to become her distraction from her own tired life, a doorway to freedom. To come into his bed. With liquor always on the sill by the bed, they ruffled in the covers, music too loud on the speakers. And after, his sweet gestures: the bending of his head to her lips, so close she could read the marks near his hairline, or yet, the unexpected reach of his hand to twirl her hair in his fingers, or in turn, his naked and cold body helping her to retrieve her clothes in the dark. A woman can forget everything.

VII

He shook. She remembers this most. How he shook and sweat. His eyes closed to focus on her own pleasure. He worried, confessed to her, "It takes me time to feel comfortable. I don't have sex very often." Their knowing of each other unwieldy and slow. His body so beautiful in its girth, the rounded belly, broad shoulders, hairless chest, large hands. He cooked her broccoli. They drank red wine. He told her about college, taught her about black history, rap, anarchism. She looked at his books as he eagerly paced around the room, picking them off the shelves to show her. It was important for him to impress her with his choice of literature. She noticed stories of crime and death and darkness, matched by his black hair and droop of shoulders as if he hid his true nature behind the equivocation: who was this woman and why was she here? After, they cleaned themselves. They dressed, sped down the road to radio, sex in their hair and dried on their thighs.

VIII

She loves the window in her bedroom. She loves it for the light it portrays onto the wood floor, onto the bed sheets, onto her hands. It's concrete. It's shadows. It's silver like lightning. She loves the light through her window like she loves the light that flashed briefly in the night, through the trailer window, a signal that he'd come, that first time. The ways that night had light: the glow of the radio lamp like a soft bronze, his headlights, his head lamp, her lighter against the cigarette she smoked, a sliver of moon just so, the eyes of the animal that watched her kneeling in the frosted grass. Later, days later, after their sex, she sits on the deck of a California river, vodka running through her body, and a cigarette dropping its ashes on the wood, and the light comes through the redwoods, and she takes its warmth and feels him in her distance, the birds slapping the water like some impressive affair meant to move her, like some taunt or jab at her indiscretion.

IX

In the end, it's the wind she's courting, its sudden behavior like the attention of a man, a wooing, the desperation of pleasure, a satisfactory way to imagine the day. Yes, the wind in its arrival is something like a man bringing her a drink. Or the way it can take away everything if you want it to. She sat at the window and waited, the trees already changing their clothes to something gold and beautiful. She waited for the moon and the wind to take her into its grip. She waited for a long time but there was nothing.

35

Home, As It Were

—Lavender, *Lavandula angustifolia*

It won't be home any longer, that tub of iron and porcelain, perched on bricks and the grey blue stone that we lay down ourselves with paste and effort and hope. The children bathe with lavender and soap, boats too, plastic cups, little men with overalls, a tiny brush for their fingers I bought at a market in a city I don't remember. Our daughter's auburn hair is always tangled, long to her hips, covering her eyes like it's her own cloak, a small room for her to shadow in. That's what she prefers. When I find her scattered in the dark reading books without light, I never hear a sound except a melody breezed from her lips in whispers. We never brush her hair—why?—we argue over how and when to trim something that has never been trimmed. Sometimes brown water runs from the fixture and we open the drain for it to swirl away—when the pipes freeze and warm again, and the water runs like bark. There is a way to notice the walls of rust and how they color our son's face when he tunes out a new song that tells the battle between the tulips and marigolds as if these flowers would ever disagree, perhaps over something as simple as the terrain of beauty. This home will not be home any longer, not like it was when we stripped the walls of rot, took up the plastic floor and threw it to the hill of thistle and grass. It won't be home like when we hung the Mexican gourds and wood from the bathroom ceiling, opening the window to the creek just a bit now full from the fall storm. Not in this time of rupture, all the beauty forgotten now, home just an untenable and fragile definition of residence, where staying is no longer a likelihood, where the nuances of our broken marriage become a story embedded into these hills. I'll fill the tub again and again, washing our daughter's hair with blossoms from our garden, the calendula, lavender, or sage we planted together on a Sunday afternoon when the dirt was new and so were we. I'll take the brush, smooth the hair down her back until it falls straight and plenty with just the edges curled in a hint of apricot, maybe coconut, a scent that will linger as the day ends and the crickets start up and the shadows appear on the tile floor, all the strands of her hair finally tidy, smooth, without snarl, without knots.

Part Three: Return

"*Propensities and principles must be reconciled by some means.*"

—Charlotte Brontë

36

Everybody Knows This is Nowhere

—Western Redcedar, *Thuja plicata*

When I think of the radio man now, I think of Neil Young first: how the radio man's eyes lit up when we appraised the genius of Young's melodies—nostalgia and grunge mixed with a dark abdomen of story. How I told him my own stories: of young love, pick-up trucks, and crazy horses; of smoking weed in my bedroom when I was sixteen listening to *Harvest* again and again, how the music was like grit and spirit; of Neil on stage, his music stunning me under the moon; of wishes like this one where he and I could sit on a hill of grass or on the hood of his car, drink beer, listen to Neil until the engine went cold or the transmitter stopped working, or the sun rose, but mostly, I remember the paper napkins: the images of playful snowmen with red caps and carrot noses printed against a blue snowflaked sky, the tissue folded in half next to the thrift store plates on which he served me broccoli and sausage matched with red wine in mugs and what was on the radio even? I can't remember, a fact which frustrates me now because between us, back then, music was everything.

That night, to my children, to Josh, I was with a friend in town, sharing drinks at a local bar on a Tuesday, but to be true, I had left the school board meeting early to drive through a storm to the radio man's one-room cabin in the woods. I'd hired a babysitter to stay with the children while Josh attended a gathering just down the road from where I would quietly disrupt our arrangement of devotion. *It's the woman in you that makes you want to play this game.* Would I pass Josh's truck in the dark? Would he wonder why I was driving in the wrong direction, away from town, toward the mountains, not going home? As I approached the darker elevation, the rain surged and the light fell away. I passed a few scattered homes, thinking their walls contained mothers settling their children into bed, whispering them stories, telling them *I love you.* I chased the storm, something stirring in the violence of clouds and water, turned the radio to an audible high, for harmony and mood, to stifle my hesitation. The wreck of music filled the car—*the world is turning, I hope it don't turn away,* the minor chords evoking a certain melancholy, a drama playing out here and now, just as I had imagined: I was going to meet a man, a man distanced from my own orthodoxy, and I would become like him, a rebel in an off-grid shack thrust into the hillside on the edge of government wilderness, living alone in a paradise. *Doesn't mean that much to me to mean that much to you.*

There with him, in his home, awkward, we ate dinner and it wasn't long before the wine took me to his bed. Every so often the lights flickered. Or sometimes they'd go completely and we'd leave it that way. Reach for each other in the dark. But on this night, the music became a resonance of our impulses, a soundtrack to our affair—we needed the tempo to hold us—so he left bed flushed and warm to crank the engine in the shed out back, his body awake to the wind and rain, trembling with cold when he came back to me. In bed, we'd stop and talk: of misogyny in hip hop, other countries like Denmark, and what it means to own a cat. He was due to go on the radio at ten. It was 9:52. He didn't seem to care. He concentrated on pleasing me, perspiration dotting his forehead, his back thin with sweat, eyes shut in pleasure or concentration I couldn't tell, though I watched him go: he was determined to make me feel good. To last. Sing low, I wanted to whisper, but I surveyed his face instead—*a perfect stranger like a cross of himself and a fox*—always shifty, nervous, quiet.

She could drag me over the rainbow.

Finished, we raced in separate cars down the rural highway, the radio station just five miles down the road, hidden in the pines, and a famous anarchist was there when we arrived playing exquisite instrumentation over pirated airspace. The anarchist shared my birthday, May 23, and so I stayed a while. He told me stories of the world changing direction, astrology and Geminis, pagan theosophy, and Judeo-Christian esotericism, which I didn't know was a thing to believe in. The anarchist scratched his gray beard, nearly sixty, and sipped his canned beer, going on like a jaw until I shifted in my seat, grew bored, lit my cigarette, and went outside to the rain, to feel the storm pass over me, to consider the radio man who was sweet with his tenderness and paper napkins speaking rap and spinning dope on the mic. We kissed in the rain, the hip hop thumping out the trailer door, the famous anarchist passed out in the corner now. I had to go, though I drove slowly so I could hear him on the dial. Save the time. When I returned home—the children asleep, Josh too—I stripped off my wet clothes, lay naked under a quilt, and plugged in my headphones, the radio man syncing the rhapsody of bass and beautiful struggle on the tuner, my fingers marked with a blend of scent like rain and smoke and pine. *Tell me lies later,* the betrayal a real thing I could not name.

37

Divorce

—Rufous Hummingbird, *Selasphorus rufus*

At the split of evening, when the ryegrass of summer appears
lengthened and tall like ballet dancers (as in: graceful sway, physique
toned, latticed hair), when the hum of each insect and every
pinwheeled flower is the string quartet that allows the trunks their
quiver, I think about our daughter, Ava, and the way she flicks her
finger and dances her shoes to the light that exists within her. She's
only four, but still, she knows how to untether the knots that have
tightened between us with just a small tilt of her head. Or grin. She
would like this place where I sit to reference the sky. Here, over a
lonely and distant spring, the seed heads have plumped, heavy now
for the summer break. Here, an Egyptian cat perches in the accidental
meadow, a place misplaced on the side of the highway where I now
live. It waits for a mouse or squirrel to dash from the barn. Too, a
makeshift laundry line stretches near, the scent of lemon, grapefruit
full on the damp sheets. The sun has disappeared behind the
mountain, dimming the tips of each seed head in this new night,
shadows going black near the edge. A strand of strange lilies, so
named for their crooked blooms and crimson blaze, call up the hot
air. And then, the hummingbird shows, a temporary stop in its
traverse of the yard, wings beating a million times as fast as my heart.

Why? To cast off courage into the air, like the cottonwood seeds that land on my fingers, which I want to put on my lips like powder and gloss. To taste the grit and fortitude brought down from the strength of old trees. The night Ava was born, she came wild and incandescent into my arms, into the slanted light of our living room, born through a meeting of eyes, an arching of heads, the touch of your heavy hand. We can think of it as unjust. We can bash our heads against this undoing. But I say, let's not, because the grass is strong, and it isn't so far to know that the hill we used to live on is there still, the home steady and solid, and it will always be there, with or without us. If anything, let's not fall backwards. If anything, let the hummingbird swing the grass dancers, let Ava move her hips to the melody of her own tune, leaving nothing for us but a trace of what we can only imagine.

dear son & daughter,

On an evening flush with stone skies, I watch children play on a limestone court: one, a boy with rubber boots, nearly too big and substantial as to overwhelm his tiny frame; two, a girl with pink bibs soaked to her knees, no shoes. The boy chased a ball. The girl pounced a puddle, both children clocking their own tempo to the aftermath of a summer storm, the air clear and humming with insects. As I watched them, I lamented this: they don't know their future pain and I can't save them from what they don't know. All that mattered were the simple things they sought: splash and puddle, catch and mitt, that place, that time. These children, this play, makes me think of you, how I might try to protect you from the world's inevitable sting.

{pause}

If I could, I might explain something of this life by picking a handful of chamomile from the hard dirt out back where the pigs live, crumple the buds in my hand so I can smell the earth, place them in a copper bowl, watch the flowers dry and break over days that run. I could bring you to the bowl, show you how the world grows and dies this way, the alloys eroding a patina of emerald and salt over our fingers as we touch the stems, creating an architecture of color that will rinse away only in the tub. So much color that will always leave us. I'd say, I remember a house in the mountains where I lived as a girl,

where the devil hid in a rock pile, where the river fell down like a
furious puppet whose strings had broken free, bringing pieces of
cooled basalt to where I stood at a juncture of earth and river. How I
wanted to remain there in a long station of awe.

{breath}

There's this too: all of my wanting, which has always been too much,
even since the occasion of wonder on that big river, so many wants
collected into me like a trough too full to carry. Do I tell you a story of
betrayal then? Of searching for approval in a man not my husband, a
man who walked me under the moon, held my whiskey glass. We
didn't have a blanket, just a gravel road we took up into the hills, on
which we shared stories of Christmas trees, graffiti, poker. All subjects
were new. I imagined fire as my hair then, instead of the sand that it is.
A pair of carnelian stones hung from my ears, a brush of crimson on
my neck, like bits of iron and chalcedony suspended, fixed by my own
careful hands, for all that's related to touch. I imagined what I'd ever
tell you of this time, if anything.

{hush}

Maybe this: There's a mountain of stone near where we live, a matrix
of feldspar, quartz. Your father and I climbed this peak on a day
warm, after we had come together again. We could see in all
directions the mountains of California, the volcanoes, the valleys too.
On that mountain, a heaviness lifted from his chest. He wrote in the
summit book, "I fucking hate hiking, but I love my wife." A slice of
reconciliation then, after months of separation, after abandonment.
Campion, ragwort, goldenweed, saxifrage, all bloomed wild on the

pastured hills. The red cedar, too, with all of its history. I sensed you there, my children, pockets full of pebbles, your lovely hair and eyes hazel like his. You would have learned from the stone, the hills, discovered the landscape with curiosity, something we always said we wanted for you.

{wait}

Or even this: I know how it feels to look up, hope for the stars to suggest a story. Constellations are recognizable, yet not, their burn displayed over the earth, their riddle a part of their beauty.

{rest}

We can only wonder what mastery their patterns might unveil. And too, there's a bear I see in the mountains. She tumbles to the road from the dark woods, exposed on the pavement, staring down the space between us. The bear, she offers no resolution or promise of understanding. Only a reminder: it all keeps burning on and on—the patient sky, the determined stars, our urgent questions.

39

Of Origins, Elegy

—Blackberry, *Rubus fruticosus*

"I grabbed a pile of dust, and holding it up, foolishly asked for as
many birthdays as the grains of dust, I forgot to ask that they be years
of youth."
—Ovid

[Placenta]

Ava asked if we were the only animals that grew placentas. I said I
didn't know, then looked it up: hyrax, golden mole, pika, lemur. We
aren't the only ones. I think of origins, hers and mine, placental
mammals, the stars, the cross and tether of a mother and daughter. I
lament what can never begin again.

[Pop songs]

Ava knows all the words to every pop song with her little yellow shirt,
size six, with the blue flower attached, $6.99 at the box store. Her
origins: conception on Valentine's Day, maturity through the summer
and the birth in November at the waxing moon. And now, the
placenta still wrapped in a plastic bag, frozen and tucked between
chicken breasts and blueberries in the downstairs freezer. When I
return home after our separation, we'll bury the organ in the yard

beneath the maple, tucked into the earth to become matter and dirt. My origin: already satisfied here in these pages, but as in all of our years, perhaps origins recur, and then from Ovid again: "We are ever striving after what is forbidden, and coveting what is denied us." I cannot be young again, not like my daughter or my son, who knows things only boys know, how to pretend we aren't hurt. It's like panning for gold with no riches to grow the bowl.

[First Day]

We tried to build holes in the sand, what we thought were portals to another place. I wanted to believe we could step through time, transport ourselves to the high prairie of Argentina or the studded mountains of Slovenia. Somewhere new on a new day on a new year. New everything: children being children, boats on the water, return to marriage. We discussed tsunamis, earthquakes, the tidal zone, all the crustaceans and mollusks making their homes in the foreshore. From driftwood, we tucked into bend of branches then followed the pockets of air waves left on the sand, running toward the arches of rock just beyond the cliff-line. I wasn't sure if we would ever get far enough to know the feel of coral on the sea stacks.

[Preservation]

I was born in a place called Creve Coeur, so typed on my birth certificate, what translates to "broken heart" from French. I've always relished telling the world I was born in Broken Heart, Missouri as if it were entirely poetic and symbolic of some greater truth. Between birth and four, I lived in a sprawling suburb of St. Louis, in a neighborhood I want to call Briarwood. This was before we left the plain beauty of Missouri for the West, where our dreams of sun and joy would turn up empty. We should have known that California was a false narrative, an LA sky whose stars only glittered for some.

[There]

I asked Ava to tell me what she saw out the window. She said, "An ocean of blackberries." I told her of a time when I was a girl and I scrambled around in a greenbelt of woods chasing after foxes in the dark. Later, as we harvest wormwood together from the field, my fingers sticky with resin and wine, she tells me a story of two Avas, one evil, one good and their mannerisms and how they shoot up the stairs into a fort saying to everyone they encounter, "How do you do?" On a trip to the Sierra, she walks with me to Heart Lake and shudders at the fear of bears, the slope of a mountain so large, her tiny figure making way through the grass and her pink backpack on her shoulders with a charm of beads hanging from the strap. We can't go back, but can build from the places we are. We can bring forward a sense of time from the geology or rock face of the mountain, something like radiance.

[Scaffold]

The artist Ben Butler sculpts cedar into rounds and snakes, then builds monuments of wood, structured like a matrix of rows and columns, towering over a room, as if from an emergence of roots, small poplar action that builds consequence and grandeur. There's intricacy and attention in his work, abstraction too, but nonetheless, with the material and substance of wood, the art becomes something authentic, as a reflection of the patterns in nature. All from a genesis of his own. In one particular sculpture, "Darwin's Worm," painted stone creates a shape not unlike a slug or sloth, all beckoning to starts and bloom. There's something here about strength and platforms and genesis.

[Firsts, again]

Our house sat on the edge of the Missouri woods, a diverse collection of oak and hickory, beech and elm, maybe dogwood. To me now, upon memory, those woods were a shadowy place, full of terror and possibility. I'd stand on the edge often, or slowly make my way out into the strand of trees only to be shivered back by fear. I know now the mix of trees was just that: a small woods in a neighborhood made large in a small girl's mind, like a fantasy haven of many creatures and fairy tales—Hansel and Gretel and witches with poison apples. And yet, though the forest inspired trepidation and doubt, they also held for me something special: a world of my youth shaped in wonder and dark beauty. And now, I recall those woods as tender and true as if it were just the other day I stood on that line of trees beckoning those Ozark fireflies into my palms.

[Pleiades]

I bought Ava a small necklace at the center of which hung a charm with the pressed shape of the Pleiades against her chest. Blue with the stars. The cluster is the most obvious to the eye, governed by luminosity. Like my daughter. Dust reflects from the nebulous part of the interstellar medium. This constellation is of the divine seven sisters. Ava, like bird, or life, or a variation of Eve.

[Puddles]

When she was two, she joyed in puddles, tickling her way to these small ponds in winter, in the middle of any lot or drive. She tumbled around our yard and gravel, picking up worms and placing them in the grass, singing, "I'm trying to save them." Why?—to preserve life, origins, vitality, so important to her. Oh yes, place.

[Age]

I lived by the beach once and used to make my own clothes from gingham squares I cut in the front yard next to the garden with peas and shallots. I went to a bar with Josh and Maurice played "Don't Worry, Be Happy" on the keyboard, sipping mulled wine every so often. I wondered if he was lonely. I bought drugs off a stranger, taking a moral inventory of those people who hid in dark places selling drugs, just as night tipped over backwards. I fell in love with a DJ once who played bass heavy techno-music in the woods on speakers programmed for echo and sound. It's not the only time I loved a DJ. I ran away once with my adolescent friend, but to run is to pass quickly or smoothly in a particular direction. To go one way. To not look back. I don't think we really knew what that meant. I still don't.

[Porcupine]

Ava asked me: "Do you know how to hug a porcupine?" You put on a hundred gloves and gather yourself from the belly to wrap your gloved hands on the spines.

40

(And amid much subdued hope there was a bit of gladness in me.
—Rilke)

Letter to Lou Salomé (3):

Say first, there was a woman who cooked animal bones, sailed small
boats, let an artist carve a tattoo on her back of birds or some other
inked drawing, I can't tell, I haven't seen it close enough to say. Say
second, that Josh took her into our bed, the bed our son and daughter
lay in after they were born, with the screen print of a leaf framed in
myrtle on the wall colored salmon. My desk there still. With books.
My things. Say third, she put on a bracelet of mine in the bathroom,
or peed in our toilet, used my brush, looked in the mirror at her
reflection, threw her hair back, smiled. Say fourth, she noticed my
wedding ring on the sill, next to his, rings we don't wear anymore. Say
fifth, she put the ring on, then thought better of herself, placing it back
where it should stay, there next to the rocks we collected on the sand.
Say sixth, she returned to our bed, where she must have curled herself
around him, her sex on my sheets. Say seventh, she woke up and he
made her coffee. Say eighth, she picked up our children's books in
the corner, perhaps the one about all the things in the world we see,
the one our son can now read to us about beaches and rain and
families who sing. Say ninth, he kissed her, maybe as he went out the

door to sell vegetables, with tenderness, adoration, the way he used to kiss me. Say tenth, she walked through my garden with the lavender, the penstemon. Say she picked a bud on her way out. Say she ran her fingers over the lupines. Say she drove away down our road, put her sunglasses on, turned the radio up, admired the peas in the greenhouses, or the piles of trees rotting now where we left them once, those trees we said we'd never cut. Say she looked up to the house as she rounded the corner, to the red barn, the fields.

*

It's like a shudder now. I think of *The Little Prince,* a treasured book I read in my high school French class, "To become spring, means accepting the risk of winter. To become presence, means accepting the risk of absence."

*

There's a song by Jeffrey Martin, "Coal Fire," that rises up from the ground like a farmers' plow lifts the dirt, a symphony of fiddle, piano, guitar, and vocals that whines like a dying coyote. A song resonant and sonorous, both harmonically and emotionally. Also, a devastating kind of sad. The song examines a complex interior life, a haunting story of loss and desperation, a melody with a moment like this: "You'd said that I could stay here/open my chest for just you to see/all these acres of quiet fire/that are burning down in me." Our quiet acres burned, and from the remnants all that remained was hurt, jealousy, a word that elicits a blanch or flinch. Jealous comes from the word zealous: or from the Swedes, to be black sick, which prompts me to think of decay, of the character of your soul festering in black thoughts, all in destruction of welfare and joy. But is that too bleak? So this, I imagined tearing her apart in ways that I had never thought possible— and when all I wanted was for us to explore the intimacies of other people. It's ironic. This jealousy. Simone de Beauvoir wrote, "Jealousy is not contemptible—real love has beaks and claws." Not a destructive behavior then, but an asset perhaps, a certitude that a specific love is authentic, true. I was jealous because I loved and if I loved, then I loved Josh.

*

Lou, I told Josh the universe was asymmetrical. This truth astonished me: nature was askew, lopsided, just a bit off by one small piece of matter. I had always assumed that balance and accord, symmetry and harmony were the rules that governed. But I suppose that's why I left to begin. I needed to discover something unfamiliar about life—that it's tilted, off-balance, that everything we do is coarse and uncertain. I told this to him on the phone, but broken symmetry to explain anything didn't interest him. He said, of course, all of nature is off, rowed with uneven boundaries. Look: the shell spirals only one way, the fiddler crab has one large claw, the other small, and the waybill grows a beak too strange to be plane, its curves crooked and just. The sponge channels and pores with its external asymmetry. Coral colonies too. They spawn an incongruity. What of the butterfly then, or moth, the beetle? The bi-lateral beauty of a human body? Leaves, when folded, rarely match. I knew we couldn't be a mirror—that I was something akin to a loose fox, he, a noble horse. Could we align? Or was she a better match?

I thought then the mountains could hold us, that they could act as a
container for our family, but the hills failed to sustain, so I moved
elsewhere. For six months of winter and spring into summer, I lived
on the side of a two-lane highway in a mobile trailer with an Egyptian
cat named Honey, several succulent desert plants, and a friend who
offered me a way out. How to describe this trailer: a gray tin of a
home with leaking roof and shower raised above the floor so that I
had to step into it, something like a small mountain, all rectangular
with mold in the corners and a small window screened to the yard. A
lonely house. An outcast house. What should have been a remnant. I
shuffled around the edges of this place with conviction: I was free,
from children, from marriage, from the relentless push of farming,
keeping an anarchist lover who lived in an off-the-grid cabin in the
woods. I could call my day the way I wanted to with a diverse
soundtrack of soul, tempo, jazz, punk filling the empty space where
my family had been, Josh, the two children. I smoked on the pallet
porch, the music overwhelming the exterior hum of the world,
shutting it all out, the lyrics of each song a match to my internal
questions, the trailer surrounded in wet pig manure, nothing growing
but a bedraggled weed here and there. Pools of urine. Mud thick
enough to sink knees into. A gravel drive with trash all around. A
plastic bag I'd been meaning to pick up for days, yet still I didn't. How
much nothing there was. I drank too much. I ate too little. Music was
the only thing that held me in one place. Victor Hugo wrote, "Music
expresses that which cannot be put into words and that which cannot

remain silent." So then: the in-between, the intermediate where confusion collides with confidence. There was the barely audible river nearby. A broken down milk parlor. Highway cars. Skull of a deer. That place: an adopted fiction of a home. Even at night, when the sounds of a different farm rose up to the ceiling fan, and I shuddered from the crack of thistle out the window, I wanted to bring him back to me. I know now I had to leave in order to see that vestige of a platinum moon in a fresh sky. Without him.

*

That summer, I often went to the junction of creek and river, where a dam created a cascade of water and rock and places to swim. In those long afternoons of arduous reconciliation, the days when I didn't know if he loved me, or her, or wanted me back, or didn't. Every day that summer, I'd pack my cloth bag with towels, beer, water, and take the children through the willow and brush, hot and supple summer, to the rocks where we'd linger until evening. I'd smoke and watch them. I'd cry maybe. I could never rest. The children knew my pain. They'd known it for so long—the months of living apart from their father, sharing a bed with their mother, toys stacked in boxes, clothes shoved in bags. Everything temporary, awaiting some new departure that never came. Ava, our daughter, was four then, and together we'd tramp down the slope of creek to the water. One day she turned to me:

    —Mama, I'm sorry you are having such a hard time.
    —Thanks, Avie.

—Maybe you should know I love when you smile, she said, grabbing the branch of a tree to steady her descent.

—Thanks. I love your smile too.

—Maybe you should know I talk to plants and that helps.

—How do you talk to plants?

—Well, you just sway a little bit and then you say, 'Shhhh...'

—Ok. Let's try it. Show me how.

I relied on the children, who on my birthday created an arrangement of strawberries, lavender, rosemary, rose petals, sage into a bowl, presenting the work with such affection for their mother, though their family was broken and had been for so long. The farm became a landscape of opposition, something to run away from, not to, the two of us fighting to the sunset in the front yard with the creeping light and shadow, the children huddling in their bedrooms, our son shaking from fear, unable to get warm. I never ate the strawberries. Or I might have later, laying on the grass under the great stars wishing for some way to sweeten the loss.

*

I failed to become the kind of woman I hoped to be, because of obligation. Of duty, or love, or morality. I cannot say for sure.

*

I want to say now, in this spring of return and season, I want to go and find the wildflowers in that spot in the desert we used to go, in the Mojave, under and between the mesquite and juniper, in the mountains of granite that created a repository for our attachment. We could take apart the desert tissue, connecting our hands, thick with sand, find pieces of me and parts of him in the buds and our nails, parts that have flown alone, parts that have stayed, all now composed together like an orchestration of desert wild. We could join together in this temporary home of black scrub and hopsage. We could take it all in. He could tell me the story again, of the creosote, how it can live for years without any water at all, its substance a foundation of drought. He could tell me again of its longevity, its commitment, living sometimes two hundred years alone. A matriarch, he could say, building colonies in an ecology of resilience. He could tell me again how the creosote smells like rain, that you can smell the water come off it in waves. And then we could draw in its scent, inhale the world in all of its wash, the whole crust of the wet earth rising up to meet us.

41

The Daily Intimacy

—Pacific Willow, *Salix lucida*

{*muse, flirt*} The firethorn, orange and plump, burns its weight in the sky. It's November now, the ground carrying an epitaph of sod and fruit. Each day expels a breath of frost on the cedar and willow. It's soon I will collect the rosehips in baskets for cordial or wreaths. On this day, Josh brings me a gift of candles, purchased at the market from a woman with ruby curls. She's handcrafted them, dipped the wicks into beeswax, butterscotch pillars wrapped in twine, what have become a conscious narrowing, tapers to convey flame on dark nights. He does not add a note, but hands them to me quickly, says, "These are for you." We've come now to the small gifts, the daily intimacies to recover our break.

{*dog, forgiveness*} In the summer of our return, when the heat burns our minds, our dog becomes immobilized by too many ticks burrowing into his thick fur, biting his skin, the fields of tall grass guilty of harboring the insect, causing this temporary handicap. Josh calls me to ask if I can stay with the dog through the afternoon while he works. We haven't been talking. He's been seeing the other woman, he thinks he loves her, but someone needs to be with the dog. So I go. I had nothing to do, not really. I was finishing school, living away from him, the children, the farm. The dog was sad, lying limp in the hallway, until which time Josh comes in from work, embraces me, holds me longer than I expect, begins to kiss me, touching my back under my shirt with his hands, dirty with melons or other such fruit. It is unexpected, but sends a ripple of sensation up my spine, a feeling I haven't had for so long. And for him. Lust. Desire. Want. The dog's tail begins to thump the wall. She's looking at us sideways from the floor, her eyes lit up with shine.

{*swing, lake*) His ambivalence was palpable, as sure as the moon. He couldn't trust me, or my intentions, wasn't sure if I loved him, but he invited me to canoe with the children on a lake we always loved, one that sparkled like an anchor, the backside of a beetle, a jelly bean. He had bought the canoe two summers before, as a surprise for me when I was away at a residency, so that it carried the force of our marriage. We canoed until we docked. The children played in the water and he slept on the sand, but we swung off a tree later into the water, laughing like nobody could say. We made out like teenagers in the sand, the sun burning our backs and knees. As we rowed home across to shore, he turned to me, "This is like before, but better."

{*beer, sex*} "I don't know you anymore," he said. We lay on the couch together, drinking beer to make the coming back less awkward, less unusual. A re-knowing of sorts. Like we were first dating. The children slept in a bed side-by-side in another house, ten miles down the road. I knew it would be weeks, months, maybe years before we could reclaim a situation of comfort. That night, we made love twice, the first time in months, the heat sifting through the window screens and staining the sheets, our skin. The eruption of emotion almost too much, but we were far enough away from the world that no one heard our cries. We sat on the deck after, no stars through the summer's smoke. I drove back to the children past midnight, leaving him in the doorway of the home our children were born in, the home I had chosen to leave in the dark of a winter January night.

{fences, october} Josh tells me I should write about fences, their intentions. I have never built a fence. I don't think I have the authority to write about fences having never constructed one myself. I like fences—rural fences. Beautiful, falling-down fences. Fences with tears, bulges, holes, barbed wire. I think there's something to be said here about boundaries. I think Josh is telling me something about division, or containers, or—

{typewriter, love} Josh's first farm auction and instead of irrigation pipe, which is what we need on the farm, he brings me a gift of three typewriters from 1902 as well as a pallet of 8-tracks, an 8-track player, a Polaroid camera, an adding machine, cassette tapes, and VHS, all purchased for one dollar, which he had to borrow from a farmer friend because his wallet was empty. He was so proud of his gift, knew I would love the antiquities. The goods sit in the barn still and will for a long time, I think, but it doesn't lessen the nature of the gift, the love behind such a gesture.

{*beach, women*} I travel to a house on the coast of Oregon where thirteen farm women have assembled for a few days upon the cliffs of the ocean. Where driftwood dominates the sand. I cook buttered leeks, drink wine with another farmer whose husband has had an affair with a farm employee. We exchange stories. She says to me between wine lips, "It's impossible not to be connected forever with children, a farm, everything you've been through together, everything you've created." We pour more wine, play games to the *White Album* and stay up too late making metaphors to the windows and the sea. I know she's right.

{*valentine, want*} The dog follows me to the bus stop at the end of our driveway. I wait for Everett while flipping through home loan mail, bills from credit cards, a valentine from a neighbor. It's that time of year when love comes rippling into our every day. Sweetheart candy. Poetry. St. Valentine. Celebration of courtly love. Josh is away. The children color with markers in the living room in his absence. Eat pretzels and cheese. I'm researching elegies with spring on the mind. The *Harry Potter* books roll on an endless loop on the speakers. What can an elegy be for but a time past? Which makes me think of the lover. And how Josh had to endure my dismissal of him as a man. And all this celebration of: wanting and not wanting.

{*art, margaritas*} I've become weary of making art, I tell him after therapy while we eat chips and drink margaritas at Rosa's Cantina. We talk about social media: the anxiety, isolation. We talk about my book. What I will say about us, all of this. How it will hurt. We drive to a warehouse far from the farm, from the cantina, and a strange man sells us plastic roll bags and we joke this is our date. There's something about this story I'm trying to pin, or mark out, tell here that has significance. Maybe it's the daily things you do with a companion that make up a life, that draw you closer over time. Like driving to purchase bags from a stranger.

{*dance, drinks*} I mix drinks for him now, and we dance to silly 80s ballads in the kitchen while the children build forts and manage to wreck the afternoon in play. I hope to move over the distance that broke us first, wonder whether this is ever a possibility.

{*fire/farm*} We cook outside. The willow moves in the wind. A storm is on the way. I chop wood to start a fire in the pit. The scent of garlic and meat rinses the air. We've poured wine and set the picnic table with our burgundy plates. Ava has chosen a bouquet of poppy, grass, and a rose for the centerpiece. Josh tosses the salad with oil. We try a few olives. Everett hides away under the homemade lemonade stand, waiting for an intruder or pirate. It's this: this picture of family, of these moments that belong to us, this thing that I gave away.

{*rain, walk*} While finishing the book I am writing about our marriage, I decide to take a walk on an April Sunday when the air is so cold it tinges my fingers with frost. Upon my return, it begins to rain steadily, and I am unprepared without an umbrella. The rain comes heavy quickly and I dial Josh's number, but he doesn't answer. I curse myself for leaving without a shell of a jacket to protect me. I can't enjoy the walk without the jacket. Soon, I see the headlights of our car come around the corner. He flashes them at me. He stops on the road, "Thought you might want a ride. Get in." There isn't anything else to say, so I do.

{*bar, poems*} After discussing our ten-year mark in therapy—the day we were married, the faults of our affairs—we go to the corner bar on a hot afternoon. What to do now. I order a coconut buckwheat beer and sort magnets to make a poem about thunder and time. There wasn't anything to say that we hadn't already said, except the reminder to love before we left, and to recall the rust-colored fields, the blue roof, and the gorgeous road of our devotion.

{*kale, june*} One evening before the sun recedes behind the hills, we take the Ford to one of our fields to harvest broccoli, cabbage. We go as a family, squeezed into the cab, one seat belt shared for two kids, our hands cold from the coming night. We eat crackers and make jokes. Stop for deer. We drive slow because that's what you do when your two children share the same seatbelt, and you're not in a hurry, when you've got everything right there in the small space of that flatbed. As Josh cuts broccoli, disappearing down to the other end of the field, the children run up and down the rows, grazing on their choices—kale, cabbage, kohlrabi, but mostly, kale. Ava comes to me, says, "Hold this." She hands me her leaf and lifts her arms. "I want to fly," she says and off she goes, costumed as some superhero, the front all dirtied with soil, bottom wet from the ground. "I want to fly," she screams and the sun, it goes down quick, back behind the trees, and the whole field gives way to smoke and shadow except for the neon red and blue of her costume as she ducks behind the truck and disappears.

42

On Wildness/On Forgiveness: To Tell the End

—Western Screech Owl, *Megascops kennicottii*

We find out the heart only by dismantling
What the heart knows.

By redefining the morning,
we find a morning that comes just after darkness.

We can break through marriage into marriage.

By insisting on love we spoil it, get beyond
affection and wade mouth-deep into love.

We must unlearn the constellations to see the stars.
  --Jack Gilbert

1. An owl dies in the road. Or against the fence. By the truck. We aren't sure of its death, just that its body is left for us on the gravel. We find out the heart only by holding the owl in our hands, turn it over to rub its back, touch its small beak, its frame lighter than a football, a steam iron, a book or shoe. Its eyes are half-lidded: a presage or forecast of good things to come, I hope. Maybe a reprieve from the little hurts that make up a marriage. A friend preserves the feathers, strings the claws onto twine for our son to wear around his neck, our daughter to loop around her wrist. We can break through marriage into marriage.

2. We used to talk about wildness. Now, we talk about forgiveness, what love is. We find out the heart only by breaking the tie between us, taking the responsible distance, seeing from afar what needs to be shed, of designing a path through the woods on trails never been.

3. I often go to the beach to collect rocks. It's at the wild base of the ocean, I think of Simone Weil, of her passages on grace, "Grace fills the empty spaces, but it can only enter where there is a void to receive it . . . the imagination is continually at work filling up the fissures which grace might pass." What is this grace: a crack, a chink or crevice, the heart a vessel we can fill, though we both work at this dream: arranging something new into a wrapped gift, all tucked into tissue paper with bits of sand falling out of the gaps.

4. There are versions of endings, of course. Maybe just transitions. Even if I tell the ending one way, of re-learning how to love again, by insisting on love, to open the place that is a wound, this doesn't become the end, just a pass-through. Nothing in the wild ever seems to end, though it feels that way, those long stretches of wilderness scraping on. But what does a field of dandelions in seed tell us about endings? Or the bark of a coyote or the fresh doe or the reflections of trees on water? We learn the ending by dismantling what the heart knows.

5. The owls' plumes streak gray, white, and call of an acceleration of whistles, creating an ascent of cadence. In the open woods, they hunt the rabbits and den into trees hollowed out by woodpeckers. At night I hear the owls, a low trill piercing the night. The windows are open to summer. I'm learning to listen and unlearn the stars.

6. We dine and next to us, a couple of more than eighty-five, slump to their meals. They don't talk, sometimes smile. They are very old. We are here celebrating my birthday. We are here drinking wine. I look over to them often. She says to the old man, "Remember the fish we had on our honeymoon?" Which must have been years ago, he says, a bit laughing, "Oh yes, I remember." Barely audible, their conversation ends and I wonder aloud if we'll be like them in age, moving beyond affection to something else entirely, like love.

7. Wildness from the fourteenth century: unrestrained, a frenzy, untamed. From Old High German wildi, from Old Frisian wilde, from Old Saxon wildi, related to wold, or the wooded upland. As in where we live. As in on this farm. As in this arc of wildness from the Klamath to the Rogue.

8. So forgiveness: And what is this word? For him, a war: a concerted battle of his own self with that of mine—is it possible to live together with a history tainted such as ours? With the knowledge of all that's transpired? Will it be as T.S. Eliot wrote, "After such knowledge, what forgiveness? Think now/history has many cunning passages,

contrived corridors . . ." Can we return? How to rid of the deception. Our history is redefined by breaking. It will always be there. It won't go away.

9. The rattlesnake was a shock of wildness, something we never really bothered to think about. It's not the first time we've seen one, but it's the first time it reminds me of our caution, our fear, of dismantling the calm for the sake of upheaval. In some circles, it is considered a privilege to see a snake, to attend to this wild. It defends its position, warns us with its rattle. Our dog goes close to it, but lets go, moves away. Fear makes us weak, I read. Cervantes wrote, "Fear is sharp-sighted, and can see things underground, and much more in the skies." We fear the rattlesnake because we imagine the disruption, the enormity of dying in the face of a rattlesnake. But this is an illusion. As in Josh's fear to love me again. I am the monster in the sky he's invented to occupy his pain.

10. I go to the field of salad and mayweed, the kind that covers you in rashes. I work side-by-side with the flowers. I bring him pomegranate juice, not realizing the significance of this: a representation of marriage, pomegranates thrown against a wall in celebration of union, the pieces breaking to the ground, for all the children to come forth. By insisting on love we spoil it.

11. I send a message to him of harvest, at evening, at the strawberry moon as they call it. I weep and sob over a radio show heard while

eating beans, eggs, onions, a little sauce, coffee. I sob and can't eat anymore. This thought of leaving and then returning. How he never understood.

12. I spread the owl's feathers out. I bring them forth as a way to understand that which was living, and now that which is dead. I wonder if Josh would collect my curls after death. Would he preserve them on string, hang them from the window? The owl now, instead of collapsing into the dirt, has been dismantled, taken apart, like our marriage. Is this, as Gilbert suggests, how we learn again?

13. We've forgotten how to be alone with each other, so instead we fill the space with work.

14. On "ness": a headland, a cape, a promontory, which for me are any number, but also a state of being attached to an adjective: as in uniqueness, as in forgiveness, as in tenderness, but also a township, a company, a people, a ship, an Irish princess. In the low light of a Tuesday, I lay in the half-shadowed dark, on our bed, and he comes to me, fatigued and quiet, lays down next to me and rests his chin on my shoulder, takes his arms around my chest. We lay like that, hear the sounds of evening chirp up like an orchestra of wild insects let loose on the night.

15.These things are unruly—wasps, bees, dandelion cotton, mustard, teasel. This weight of summer: the grasses overrun with seed. I haunt the apple trees. In a canoe, I drift.

16. In the car, night taking over. In the boat, the criticism deeper and more violent because of our past. At the table, a strained conversation, the lack of a soft word, or when I sit on the curb, a defiant woman whose husband cannot love her the way she wants him to. Robert Musil writes of bliss, of tenderness: "It was tenderness with melancholy which we bring to a time that belongs irrevocably to the past." The coyotes have been ranging close by—howling, shrieking, most likely in tactile arrangements, rolling on the hillside, patching down. I open all the windows for this cry of close harmony, that which is missing from my own den. I hope for a return to the tender without the despair. To forgive the past.

17. Marriage, a text essay, sent to your best friend: When your kids are gone for the night and you make romantic plans to spend time with your husband—cook dinner together, sit outside with a drink, listen to music and podcasts, converse without interruptions, watch a movie on the couch, have sex anywhere you want to—and then the mainline on the irrigation blows and your husband has to fix it by digging a six-foot hole by hand because no-one is available who has an excavator and if he doesn't dig the hole and fix the water line, all the plants in the field will die because it's going to be very hot soon and if everything dies, then you won't have any crops to sell, which means

you won't have any money either. But then, on top of it, he has to spend the rest of the evening harvesting zucchini for the farmers' market, and because no one on the crew can do it, your husband works past dark making money for the family, and when he comes in, he'll be so tired from it all that he'll fall asleep in the bath, so fuck it, you drink the special aged bottle of hard cider your apple farmer neighbors gave you, don't make dinner because what's the point, no one is even there to share it with you, and then you feel guilty for being mad and disappointed at all, so you walk the potato fields at the hour when the light scrubs the soil in bronze layers, and think the farm steals a marriage, and you want to steal it back.

18. So many things go wrong on a birthday, this celebration of birth, which is so related to dying, and then there is the middle, which is supposed to be the finest part. This year, I take a walk to the woods with Ava, the girl who steals my heart, on average, every time she opens her mouth to speak and smile. She takes me to a rock pile in a ditch of boulders and shrubs, sprinkles leaves on my hair to "make nature appear," she says, as if this were the most perfect and normal action a child should take. I think of how we drink the wild air, as Emerson suggested so many decades ago. On my birthday, we watch the swallowtails and checkerspots consume the garden. This year, Josh has forgotten my birthday, or decided against celebrating. I want him to take me somewhere and say, "I know what it's like to love and come back from that un-love, and then, to reclaim it."

19. Resilience as a word for both these "nesses" to consider: forgiveness/wildness. It's a matter of recovery, I suppose, him breaking patterns of judgement, of anger, of criticism. Of softening, of letting me in. But, I've broken him and that "ness" is difficult to bounce back from. I research resilience. I want to find someone else who has written something more beautiful than I can. James Baldwin, "Some moments in a life . . . can make up for so much in that life . . . if one can live with one's own pain, then one respects the pain of others, and so, briefly, but transcendentally, we can release each other from pain." I think there must be something to this, together in pain we are free, that togetherness/collectivity is how we cure despair, but I'm not sure the man I want back can release his/my/our pain, can dismantle what his heart knows now. But perhaps. And what of the theory of resilience: once a place is disturbed, for whatever reason, it can and does have the ability to return to equilibrium, to what is stable. So in wild. So in marriage.

20. { }

Appendix

Of Farm Ecology
{if not for these, then this place would empty of the beauty that calls
up the word home}

Trees
Canyon Live Oak, *Quercus chrysolepis*
Black Oak, *Quercus kelloggii*
Wild Forest Apple, *Malus sylvestris*
Douglas Fir, *Pseudotsuga menziesii*
Madrone, *Arbutus menziesii*
Oregon Ash, *Fraxinus latifolia*
Big Leaf Maple, *Acer macrophyllum*
Ponderosa Pine, *Pinus ponderosa*
Western Redcedar, *Thuga plicata*
Ornamental Cherry, *Prunus avium*

Shrubs
Manzanita, *Arctostaphylos uva-ursi*
Pacific Willow, *Salix lucida*
Blackberry, *Rubus fruticosus*
Oceanspray, *Holodiscus discolor*
Oregon Grape, *Berberis aquifolium*
Western Hazelnut, *Corylus cornet*
Poison Oak, *Toxicodendron diversilobum*

Flowers
Douglas Iris, *Iris douglasiana*
Warrior's Plume, *Pedicularis densiflora*
Wild Rose, *Rosa acicularis*
Wood Rose, *Rosa woodsii*
Yarrow, *Achillea millefolium*
Oregon Lily, *Lilium columbianum*
Trillium, *Trillium ovatum*
California Poppy, *Eschscholzia californica*
Lavender, *Lavandula angustifolia*

Siskiyou Mariposa Lily, *Calochortus persistens*

Grasses
Nevada bluegrass, *Poa secunda*
Tall Fescue, *Festuca arundinacea*
Timothy, *Phleum pratense*
Orchardgrass, *Dactylis glomerata*

Birds
Western Scrubjay, *Aphelocoma californica*
Mountain Chickadee, *Poecile gambeli*
Steller's Jay, *Cyanocitta stelleri*
American Robin, *Turdus migratorius*
Western Bluebird, *Sialia mexicana*
Wild Duck, *Anas platyrhynchos*
Canada Goose, *Branta canadensis*
Great Blue Heron, *Ardea herodias*
Rufous Hummingbird, *Selasphorus rufus*
Red-Tailed Hawk, *Buteo jamaicensis*
Turkey Vulture, *Cathartes aura*
Barn Swallow, *Hirundo rustica*
Violet-Green Swallow, *Tachycineta thalassina*
Red-winged Blackbird, *Agelaius phoeniceus*
Common Raven, *Corvus corax*
Spotted Towhee, *Pipilo maculatus*
Cedar Waxwing, *Bombycilla cedrorum*
Pileated Woodpecker, *Dryocopus pileatus*
Red-breasted Sapsucker, *Sphyrapicus ruber*
Northern Flicker, *Colaptes auratus*
Western Screech Owl, *Megascops kennicottii*

Animals/Reptiles/Amphibians
Black-Tailed Deer, *Odocoileus hemionus*
Skunk, *Mephitidae*
Black Bear, *Ursus americanus*
Cougar, *Puma concolor*
Bobcat, *Lynx rufus*
Coyote, *Canis latrans*
Western Gray Squirrel, *Sciurus griseus*

Red Fox, *Vulpes vulpes*
Raccoon, *Procyon lotor*
Ground Squirrel, *Sciuridae*
Opossum, *Didelphimorphia*
Rattlesnake, *Crotalus oreganus*
American Bullfrog, *Rana catesbeiana*
Pacific Treefrog, *Hyla regilla*

Crops
Arugula, *Eruca sativa*
Bokchoy, *Brassica rapa*
Tomatoes, *Solanum lycopersicum*
Eggplant, *Solanum melongena*
Sweet Peppers, *Capsicum annuum*
Strawberries, *Fragaria ananassa*
Kale, *Brassica oleracea*
Romano Beans, *Phaseolus vulgaris*
Fennel, *Foeniculum vulgare*
Sorrel, *Rumex acetosa*
Leek, *Allium ampeloprasum*
Lettuce, *Lactuca sativa*
Carrot, *Daucus carota subsp. sativus*
Onions, *Allium cepa L.*
Garlic, *Allium sativum*
Shallots, *Allium cepa*
Radish, *Raphanus sativus*
Turnip, *Brassica rapa subsp. rapa*
Spinach, *Spinacia oleracea*

& any number of other crops, insect, spider, butterfly, and other small creatures too many to list here, but the space they occupy is significant and important, and the substance of diversity and range.

Acknowledgements

I love reading the acknowledgements at the back of any book, but until now, I didn't realize how incredibly difficult it would be to write my own, that is, to sincerely thank all of the good people who have enhanced my life in so many extraordinary ways, but, here I'll try.

First, thank you to Amanda Miska and Kristine Langley Mahler at Split Lip Press for loving my book. I feel immense gratitude for your insightful and smart editorial direction as well as your patience in answering all of my stressful questions.

There are so many friends and writers who have supported me over the years. Dearest Laurie Easter, who is a saving grace, just over the ridge, in-between the pines. Andrea Blancas Beltran, thank goodness for you, my dear poet and friend. Thank you especially to Tyler Brewington, Kelly Absalom Harwood, Annie Bleecker, Mary-Kim Arnold, Mo Duffy Cobb, Lauren Banks, Shelley Elkovich, Robert Arellano, Unity Bubb-Manson, Ben Hahn, Denise Smith-Rowe, Melissa Fisher, and Jamieson Bunn. Thank you, Tracy Harding, for always being willing to listen to my bullshit. Thank you, Kathryn Figliomeni, for giving me friendship and a home where some of this book was written. To Chanel Dubofsky, are you still nervous like I am? And my deepest gratitude to Maud Macrory Powell. You know why.

To my Vermont College of Fine Arts mentors: Barbara Hurd, Larry Sutin, Bob Vivian, and Patrick Madden. Each of you gave me just what I needed at the time I needed it. I am deeply indebted to you for your mentorship and thoughtful attention to my writing. Thank you to Robert Michael Pyle for introducing me to the power of the essay and to the beauty of paying attention. Other teachers and authors who have helped and encouraged me along the way, whether they knew it or not: Annick Smith, Phil Condon, Douglas Glover, Abby Frucht, Jen Bervin, Scott Russell Sanders, David Jauss, Rob Spillman, Roz Spafford, Sue William Silverman, Jill McCabe Johnson. Thank you to all the talented writers I've shared workshop space and residencies with at Tin House, the Bread Loaf Environmental Writers' Conference, PLAYA, and Art Smith. You've impacted me in ways you can't imagine.

To Cari Luna, Robin Marie MacArthur, and Jill Talbot for taking the time to read the book, for inspiring me as a writer, and for your kind and considerate words.

To Angelisa Russo, Amy Bull, and the many others who have contributed their time to helping this book come into the world.

Thank you to the editors of the following publications in which some of these writings first appeared, often in very different form: *Terrain.org, River Teeth, The Collapsar, The Bellingham Review, Sweet, Mid-American Review, Cobra Lily Review, Numero Cinq, Guernica, Split Lip Magazine, This Magazine, Wildness,* and *Hobart.*

To the Siskiyou Mountains where this book is placed.

To my parents, Don and Susan, for challenging me always.

To my brother, Don, whom I'll follow on the trail anywhere.

To my children, Everett and Ava. This book is for you.

To Josh. I'm not an easy one, so thank you for your love.

In love and wildness,

Melissa

NOW AVAILABLE FROM

This. This. This. Is. Love. Love. Love.
By Jennifer Wortman

The Future is Here and Everything Must Be Destroyed
By Colette Arrand

The Quiet Part Loud
By Tyler Barton

Hungry People
By Tasha Coryell

General Motors
by Ryan Eckes

For more info about the press and our titles, visit our website:
www.splitlippress.com

Find us on Facebook:
facebook.com/splitlippress

Follow us on Twitter:
@splitlippress

53080783R00144